IQ
Intelligence questions
For
Middle school students
High school students

Mathematic Logic

authorHOUSE®

AuthorHouse™ LLC
1663 Liberty Drive
Bloomington, IN 47403
www.authorhouse.com
Phone: 1-800-839-8640

Published by AuthorHouse   09/02/2014

ISBN: 978-1-4969-3189-4 (sc)
ISBN: 978-1-4969-3188-7 (e)

IQ-intelligence Question

This IQ – book has been prepared for secondary school and high school students, with the aim of developing the problem solving skills of the mind. These tests result in the development of learning skills, making deductions from what they have learnt, applying these to new situations, analytical thinking and finding solutions. General ability tests provide information on the degree of benefit which can be derived by a person from education. These tests cause the potential of students with superior abilities to stand out, and for them to recognize the contributions they can make to themselves and the community. Some parents and guardians are able to learn the IQ and intelligence capabilities of their children through these tests.

The book generally consists of questions on numbers, processes, tables, platforms and the relationships of these with each other. The aim here is to attempt to form a relationship between verbal questions and numbers, without frightening the students. The objective is to create a love of mathematics by setting off from verbal questions. The second part of the book contains more questions in particular on numbers, processes, and the relationships between numbers and shapes. The aim here is to use the basic mathematical processes to develop the capability of students to think quickly.

IQ tests are tests of tendency and talent which measure the intellectual strength of individuals. They are comprised of different tests, including verbal, visual and numerical. These tests measure the abilities of students to retain information within their memory in the short term, and their problem solving skills.

Due to these tests we are able to learn the capabilities of students in the areas of:

- thinking quickly
- problem solving
- deductive reasoning
- ability to carry out fast and faultless procedures with regard to numbers
- ability to notice details within a short time
- ability to detect inconsistencies
- ability to carry out procedures using numbers
- ability to compare shapes and find matching ones
- ability to work with numeric concepts

Tayyip Oral

Contents

NUMBERS

1. 3,5,7,11,13,?
    What number should replace the question mark?
    a)14   b)15   c)16   d)17   e)18

    answer :d

    solution: all of the numbers in the progression are prime numbers. the prime number after 13 is 17.

2. 1,4,9,16,?

    What number should replace the question mark?
    a)17   b)20   c)25   d)26   e)30

    answer:c

    solution: In the progression the numbers are square of consecutive numbers .5X5=25

3. 1,8,27,64,?

    What number should replace the question mark?
    a)100   b)125   c)130   d)140   e)160

    answer:b

    solution: in the a progression , the numbers are cubes of 1,2,3,4, and the number after 4 is
    5X5X5=125

4. 36,72,108,144,?
    What number should replace the question mark?

    a)180   b)170   c)160   d)150   e)140

    answer:a

    solution: in the progression the numbers are multiples of : 36, .
    144+36=180

5. 34,52,16,43,?
    Instead of the question mark what number should next?
    a)70   b)64   c) 36   d)63   e)72

    answer:a

    solution: in the progression t h e   total of the numbers are :
    3+4=7,5+2=7,1+6=7,4+3=7,7+0=7

6. 2;4;3;9;4;16;5;25;6;?
    Instead of the question mark what number should next?

    a)30 b)32   c)34   d)36   e)38

    answer:d

    solution: the second b number of the set are squares of the previous number .6*6=36

7.   1,9,25,49,?
        Instead of the question mark what number should next?

        a)71 b)61 c)51 d)41 e)81   **answer:e**
        solution: the numbers in the progression are squares of successive odd numbers:
        1,3,5,7,9,9*9=81

8.   12,23,,45,67,78→21,?,54,76,87
        Instead of the question mark what number should listed?
        a)32 b)24 c)23 d)79 e)36
                                                                                 answer:a
        solution: the numbers on the right side of the arrow are the inversed numbers of the left side
              numbers .

9.   21,23,34,45,67→2,6,12,20,?
        Instead of the question mark what number should be listed?
        a)23 b)28 c)30 d)36 e)42
                                                                                 answer:e
        solution: the numbers on the left side of the arrow are multiplied by each digit and then, they are
        written on the right side of the arrow. 6*7=42

10.   if a = 5   then 22 = ?
        a)4a   b)3a c)4a+1   d)4a+2   e)3a+3
                                                                                 answer:d
        solution: a=5 , 22=20+2=4*5+2=4a+2

11.   if 3a+3b=c t h e n   27a+27b=?

        a)4c b)6c c)7c d)8c e)9c
                                                                                 answer:e
        solution.   27a+27b=9*3a+9*3b=9(3a+3b)=9c

12.   a: 42   61   82   75   91
        b: 2   5   6   2   ?
        Instead of the question mark what number should there ?
        a)2   b)3   c) 6   d)7   e)8
                                                                                 answer:e
        solution: the difference in a progression are written to   b progression .9-1=8

13.   46,73,91,82, ?
        Instead of the question mark what number should there?
        a)55 b)63 c)38   d)85   e)54
                                                                                 answer:a
        solution: in the progression , the sum of the two numbers is
           : 10 ,.5+5=10

14.   7,12,17,22,27,?
      Instead of the question mark what number should there ?

      a)32   b)33   c)30   d)36   e)38   **answer:a**

      solution: in the progression numbers are increased by 5. 27+5=32

15.   44,41,38,35,?
      Instead of the question mark what number should there ?

      a)34   b)32   c)31   d)28   e)25   **answer:b**

      solution:in the progression the numbers are decreased by 3 ;.35-3=32

16.   which number does not belong?

      a)21   b)15   c)10   d)6   e)17   **answer:e**

      solution: choices a,b,c,d are divisible numbers .only 17 is a prime number. it can
      only divided itself .

17.   which number does not belong?
      a)1OO   b)121   c)144   d)169
      e)132   **answer:e**
      solution: a,b,c,d are square of 1O;11;12;13; numbers. However,132 is not square of anything .

18.   Find the difference below.
      a) triangle   b) rectangle   c)square   d)paralelogram   e)integral
                                                                answer:e
      solution. the names of a,b,c,d options are geometric shapes .integral is not a shape.

19.   Find the difference below
      a)area   b)volume   c)side area   d)circle   e)logarithm
                                                                answer:e
      solution;a,b,c,d are subjects in geometry . logarithm is a subject in
      algebra.

20.   Find the different below:
      a)angles   b)triangles   c)siymmetry   d)cylinder   e)limit   **answer:e**

      solution :options are subjects of geometry .limit is an

      algebra subject.

21. A progression: 43   62   73   84
     B progression: 12   12   21   ?
     Instead of the question mark what number should come next?
     a)16   b)15   c)14   d)12   e)10

     answer:a
     solution: at the A progression the numbers are multiplied and then, written in progression.B.
     4*3=12;   6*2=12 ; 7*3=21;   8*4=32

22. A progression: 72   84   93   41   73
     B progression: 5   4   6   3   ?
     Instead of the question mark what number should come next in the sequence ?
     a)1   b)2   c)3   d)4   e)5

     answer:4
     solution: the difference between the numbers progression A are written in progressions B.
     7-2=5;   8-4=4 ;   9-3=6;   4-1=3 ;   7-3=4

23. A progression: 22   63   97   997   9999
     B progression: 2   3   4   ?   6
     Instead of the question mark ,what number should come next ?
     a)5   b)6   c)7   d)8   e)9

     answer:a
     solution: the total of the numbers in   progression A, are equal to the square of the numbers in progressiov B.
     2+2=2*2; 6+3=3*3 ;   9+7=4*4 ,   9+9+7=25=5*5

24. a: 9,13,17,21,x
     b: 7,13,19,25 y
     x+y=?
     a) 47   b) 46   c) 45   d) 56   e) 48

     answer:d
     solution: the numbers in   progressionsin A, are increased by 4. x=21+4=25, in the b progression
     the numbers are increased 6 by 6 .

     y=25+6=31   x+y=25+31=56
25. a: 6,11,16,21,26,x
     b: 8,11,14,17,20,y   what does (x+y) equal=?
     a)54   b)52   c)50   d)48   e)49

     answer:a
     solution. In the A progression the numbers are increased by 5 . x=26+5=31 in the B progression
     the numbers are increased 3 by 3 .
     y=20+3=23   x+y=31+23=54

26. 14,20,17,23,20,26,23,29,?
     a)24   b)25   c)26   d)27   e)28

     answer:c
     solution: in the number progression 6 is added to one number. ,the 3 is subtracted from the next
     number. which means positive six, negative 3,
     29-3=26

27. a: 123   441   883   148   992
     b: 7   9   19   13   ?

     a)20   b)21   c)22   d)23   e)24

     answer:a

     solution. The total of the digit in progression A, are written in progression B. 9+9+2=20

28. a   b   c
     3   4   11
     6   4   23
     8   2   15
     9   3   ?

     a)23   b)24   c) 26   d)28   e)27

     answer:c

     solution: in the A progression numbers are multiplied by. numbers in the B progression. Then next one is subtracted from the number and written in C

29. a   b   c
     12   14   8
     62   13   12
     93   25   19
     27   78   ?

     a)16   b)17   c)18   d)19   e)24

     answer:e

     solution. The totals of column A and B are written in the C column
     2+7+7+8=24

30. a: 6   4   8   10   12
     b: 9   2   16   25   ?

     a)36   b)32   c)30   d)28   e)27

     answer:a

     solution: the number in progression A is divided by to two and the. square of the found number is written in progression B.

31. 92Δ11

     64 Δ10

     73 Δ 10

     88 Δ ?
     a)16   b)15   c)14   d)13   e)12

     answer:a

     solution: the digits are added together on the left side of the triangle and the answer is written on the right side. 8+8=16

32. 9 Δ 3→13

8 Δ 2→14

3 Δ 3→11

6 Δ3→?

a)1   b)2   c)3   d)4   e)5

answer:b

solution: the function of Δ symbol is division. The number an the left is divided to the by number on the right

6:3=2

33. 2 Δ1→3

3 Δ1 →8

4 Δ1 →15

5 Δ1→?

a)21 b)22   c)23 d)24   e)25

answer:d

solution: the differences between the squares of numbers are made . 5*5-1*1=25-1=24

AΔB→C ,C=A.A-B.B

34. 3612©→3

4816©→ 3

5117©→3

6416©→?

a)1   b)2   c)3   d)4   e)5

answer:d

solution. The first 2 digits are divided by the following 2 digit.ABCD©→X ,X=AB:CD, 64/16=4

35. 84©→16

64©→12

28©→ 8

98©→?

a)36   b)32   c)28   d)24   e)18

answer:a

solution. the numbers on the right side of the symbol © are multipled by each other, and the result is written to right side of © symbol. Ab ©= x , x=(a.b):2 ,(9*8):2=36

36. 123456→612345→561234→ 456123→ ?

a)123456 b)612345 c)345612 d)621345   e)561 ab234

solution:

answer:c

37. 23;45→5,9
     12;51→3,6
     43,61→7,7
     32,15→?,?

     a)5,5 b)6,7 c)7,6   d)5,6 e)6,5

     answer:d

     solution. if ab;cd→xy then a+b=x, c+d=y if x= 3+2=5, y= 1+5=6

38. 23 Δ 14→6;4
     34 Δ 15→12;5
     45 Δ53→20,15
     67 Δ73→?

     a)42;21   b)45;21   c)13;10   d)13;21   e)21;42

     answer:a

     solution. if ab→cd——→mn , then,   a*b=m and c*d=n makes
     6*7;7*3→42;21

39. 2Δ →5
     3Δ → 10
     6Δ→37
     8Δ→?

     answer:b

     a)64 b)65   c)66   d)67   e)68

     solution: if xΔ→y   then, y=x*x+1 so, y=8*8+1=65

40. 123456789→912345678→791234568→579123468→?
     a)8579123456 b)678912345   c)579123456 d)357912468 e)357912345

     answer:d

     solution: the last odd number of the sequence is the first digit of the next

     sequence

41. 123456789→812345679→681234579→468123579→?
     a)246813579 b)246812345 c)246413579 d)246813456 e)468123456

     answer: a

     **solution:the last even number is written at the beginning on the next
     sequence in order.**

42. 64→82
     62→35
     72→36
     43→?

     a)44   b)54   c)76   d)38   e)61

     answer:e

     solution: addition of the numbers at the right and the left of the arrow are
     equal.AB→CD , A+B=C+D
     4+3=6+1

43. 81→42
     33→91
     61→32
     22→?

     a)44   b)54   c)76   d)38   e)41

     answer:e

     solution: the multiple of the digits on the right and the left of the arrow
     symbol are the same. AB→CD then A.B=C.D

44. 82Δ71
     63Δ41
     82Δ60
     94Δ?

     a)74   b)65   c)85   d)53   e)61

     answer :e

     solution: the subtraction between the numbers on the left and the right side of arrow are the same.
     ABΔCD   A-B=C-D, 9-4=6-1=5

45. 24→42
     36→63
     64→46
     23→?
     a)32   b)22   c)42   d)21   e)52

     answer:a

     solution: the number on the right of the arrow are the inverse of
     the numbers on the left. AB→CD , A+B=C+D,

46. 25→5
     144→12
     289→17
     400→?

     a)18   b)19 c)20   d)21   e)22

     answer:c

     solution: the number on the left is the square of the number on the
     right . 20*20=400

47. 1→1
     2→8
     3→27
     4→?

     a)16   b)26   c)46   d)54   e)64

     answer:e

     solution: the number on the left is the cube of the number on the right.

48. 123 Δ→ 4
     363 Δ→12
     483 Δ→ 16
     513 Δ→ ?

     a)15   b)16   c)17   d)18   e)19

     solution. abc Δ→ x   x=ab/c   51/3=17

     Answer:c

49. a©b=a+b/a-b   if   4©3=?
     a)2   b)3   c)4   d)6   e)7

     answer: e

     solution. 4©3=4+3/4-3=7/1=7

50. a©b=(a*b+1)/a*b-1   if   8©6=?

     a)49/47   b)49/48   c)47/49   d)47/47   e) 45/49

     answer :a

     solution:8©6=8*6+1/8*6-1=49/47

51. a©b=(a*b+2)+a/b   if   10©5=?

     a)50   b)51   c)52   d)53   e)54

     answer:e

     solution: 10©5=10*5+2+10/5=50+2+2=54

52. a©b=(2a+1)/(2b-1)   if   6©4=?

     a)13/2   b)13/5   c)13/7   d)12/7   e)12/5

     answer:c

     solution. 6©4=(2.6+1)/2*4-1=13/7

53.
a	b	c
7	12	5
8	17	9
3	10	7
11	?	12

a)19   b)20   c)21   d)22   e)23

answer:e

solution. If   b=a+c   then
11+12=23

53.
a	b	c
6	2	12
7	1	7
8	3	24
4	5	?

a)18   b)19   c)20   d)21   e)22

answer:c

solution: a*b=c   then   4*5=20

54.
a:	2	4	6
b:	4	4	8
c:	1	2	3
d:	7	10	?

a)17   b)16   c)15   d)14   e)13

answer: a

solution: if a+b+c=d   then   6+8+3=17

55.
a:	2	4	6	7
b:	1	2	3	8
c:	3	9	19	?

a)57   b)56   c)55   d)54   e)53

answer:a

solution: if c=a*b+1   then

7*8+1=57

56.   kansas∆arkansas
montana∆louisiana
california∆?
a)pennsylvania   b)oregon   c)utah   d)texas

answer:a

solution: the last three letters of the states should be the same.

57. alabama→4
    alaska →3
    arkansas→4
    kansas→?

    a)5 b)4 c)3 d)2 e)1

    Answer:d

    solution: the number on the right of the arrow indicates the
    number of A used in the word on the left.

58.   ohio→2
    oklahoma→2
    oregon→2
    vermont→?

    a)1 b)2   c)3 d)4   e)5
    solution:in the names of state of letters are taken into account

    Answer:a

59. alabama→4,1,1,1
    kansas →1,2,1,2
    hawaii→1,2,1,2,
    ohio→?

    a)2,1,1   b)1,1,2   c)1,3,1   d)3,1,1   e) 4,1,1

    solution : the number indicate the amount of each
           letter is used in the word.

    answer:a

60.   alabama Δ texas→4©1

    utah   Δ kansas→1©2

    florida Δ arkansa→?
    a)1© 3   b)2©3   c)3©1   d)1© 4   e)3© 3
    solution; the numbers indicate number of the letter a in the state names

    answer:a

61.   hawaii ,illinois, minnesota ,?

    a)missouri b)montana   c)oregon   d)utah e) kansas

    solution:two of the same letter are written consecutively in the states
    name .

    answer;a

62.   texas Δ utah→1

    answer:a

    oregon Δ lowa→2

    nebraska Δ lowa→4
    mississippi Δ ohio→?

    a)7   b)6 c)5 d)4 e)3

    solution:the amount of letters per state name on the left of the Δ
    are sub tracted from those on the right.

63. alabamaΔ colorado→4+3

oregon Δ ohio→2+2

alaska Δ kansas→?

a)3+3 b)3+2 c)2+1   d)2+4   e)1+3

solution: the letter that is used the most in the state names to the left of the Δ is added to that on the right of it.   **answer:3+2**

64. texas Δ utah→20

oregon Δ ohio→24

lowa Δ kansas→?

a) 20   b)24 c) 28   d) 18   e)21

answer:b

solution: the number of letters in each state name is multiplied together..

65. lowa→utah

oregon→ alaska

kansas→?

a)nevada b)montana c texas   d) lowa   e)oklahoma

answer: a

solution: the number of letters in the state names are equal to each other.

66. montana Δ nevadaΔ oregon→2+2+2

alabama Δ arkansa Δ colorado→?<?<?

a)3+3+1 b)3+1+3 c)3+3+0   d)4+3+3   e)2+2+2

solution: the letters that repeat in each state name are added.   **answer:d**

67. arizona → indiana

florida→nevada

nebraska→?

a)alaska b)ohio c)virginia d)texas e)lowa

solution: the last two letters of each the state

names should be the same   **answer:a**

68. utah Δ lowa →l

alaskaΔ nevada→l

oklahoma Δ ohio →?

a)l b)2 c)3   d)4 e)5

answer:b

solution. The amount of letters in each state name is divided together

69.   Iowa→ triagle ,   texas→pentagon,   ohio→?

a)triangle   b)square   c)pentagon   d)hexagon   e) hexagon   **answer:b**
solution: the number of letters in state names is equal to the number of edges of the geometric shape.

70.   alaska→36
        kansas→36
        nebraska→?
        a) 54 b) 35 c)25   d) 64   e)66
                                                                        answer:d
        solution.the amount of letters in each state name is squared.

71.   Find the difference below:

        a)alabama   b)ohio   c)ariz ona   d)alaska e) oklahoma
                                                                        answer:e
        solution. the first and the last letters of each state name should be the same.

72.   alabama→1213141
        nebraska→56371891
        alaska→?
        a)121891   b)131891   c)141789   d)141789   e)151123
        solution: a=1,L=2, s=8,k=9,Alaska=121891   **answer:a**

73.   Find the difference below:
        a)bolton   b) boston   c) benton   d)brockton   e)bristol
                                                                        answer:e
        solution.;a.b,c,d are have the same ending

74.   dallas→123324
        dade→1215
        dale→?

        a)1245 b)1235 c)2351   d)1542   e)1533
                                                                        answer:b
        solution: d=1,a=2,l=3, e=5   dale→1235

75.   dayton→123456 , davis→12789, y+t+s=?

        a)17 b)16 c)15 d)14   e)13
                                                                        answer:a
        solution: d=1 ,a=2 ,y=3 ,t=4 , o=5 , n=6 ,v=8 , s=9
        y+t+s=3+4+9=16

76.   lova,alaska, utah→ 7849,1234,41464   if   l+a+s+h=?
       a)19   b)20   c)21   d)22   e)23

       answer:b
       solution. alaska consists of 6 letters which means it should be equal to the number, with 6, on the right.
       alaska→ is 41464 if a=4, l=1 ,s=6 , then   L=1 then, Lova→ 1234 is . o=2 ,v=3 the rest is represented AS utah→7849 . u=7 , t=8 ,a=4 , h=9   l+a+s+h=1+4+6+9=20

77.   ohio , utah → 4562 ,1231   ise o+a=?
       a)9 b)8 c)7 d)6   e)5

       answer:c
       solution: since the the first and the last letter of ohio are the same the corresponding , numbers of each letter are 1231 . if ohio→1231 , then o=1, h=2 ,i=3 . if utah→is 4562 then, u=4, t=5 ,a=6 o+a=1+6=7

78.   if nevada , nebraska→ 123454 ;12674894 then b+v+s=?
       a)16 b)17 c)18 d)19 e)20

       answer:b
       solution: nevada consists of 6 letters. And the number representing nevada is 123454.
       if nevada→12345 then n=1,e=2,v=3,a=4,d=5,   the numbe r representing nebraska is 12674894
       nebraska→12674894   ,n=1,e=2,b=6,r=7,a=4,s=8,k=9,a=4   ,   b+v+s=6+3+8=17

79.   texas; maine→12345;64782   x+i=?
       a)8 b)9   c)10   d)11   e)12

       answer:c
       solution. the second and the 5th letter of maine are the same. then,   texas→ 12345 ; maine→ 64782 .
       x+i=3+7=10

8O.   If arizona;oregon→1234561;527856   then i+g=?
       a)8   b)9   c)1O   d)11   e)13

       answer.e
       solution: since the first and the last letter of ari ona are the same then   ariz ona→1234561 ,
       so oregon is 527856 . i+g=3+8=13

81.   If delmar;delhi→123456;12378 then   deli=?
       a)1328 b)1238   c)1428   d)1627   e)1242

       answer:b
       solution: since delmar consists of six letters. then, delmar→123456 . then, delhi→12378 .
       deli→1238 each letter represents a number to the right of the arrow

82.   If denver;denton→ 123673;123425 then v+e+r=?
       a)1O   b)11 c)12 d)13 e)14

       answer:b
       solution. If the second and the fifth letters of denver are the same then the representing number is
       123425. If denver→123425 and denton→ 123673 then   v+e+r=4+2+5=11

83.   If eden;edna;elko→1567;1213;1234 then (e+a)/(l+o)
       a)5/12   b)6/13   c)12/5   d)13/6   e)13/5

answer:a

       solution:

       eden=1213,e=1,d=2,n=3,edna=1234,elko=1567,

       (e+a):(L+o)=(1+4):(5+7)=5:12

84.   If fargo,fenn,flora→18592,12345,1677   then (n+f)*(l-r)
       a)30   b)35   c)40   d)42   e)45

answer:c

       solution: the last two letters of fenn are the same then, and is represted by 1677 since A letter is
       the second letter of fargo and at the last in flora then, a=2., so, fargo=12345, flora 18592 .n=7, f=1,
       l=8 , r=3 (n+f)*(l-r)=(7+1)*(8-3)=8*5=40

85.   If   galax,gallup,geneva→123367,12325,189802   then, l+v+n+x=?
       a)16   b)17   c)18   d)19   e)20

answer:b

       solution: the second and the fourth letters of galax are the same. Therefore the word galax ,
       represents 12325 number. in gallup word , the third and the fourth letters are the same then, the
       gallup word represents
       123367 number , and geneva represents 189802 .   l+v+n+x=3+0+9+5=17

86.   If   hamden,hamer,hanover,→1268957,123456,12357

       a)18   b)19   c)20   d)21   e)23

answer:a

       solution: hanover consists of seven letters. then , and is represented as   1268957 . hamer of
       five letters and is represented by 12357 . the word Hamden consists of 6 letters and is represented
       by 123457   . m+n+v=3+6+9=18

87.   If   kamas,kaplan,karluk→128691,12324,125627   what does   l+u+k=?
       a)12   b)14   c)16   d)15   e)18

answer:c

       solution: in kamas the second and the fourth letters are the same. the word kamas is represented by
       12324 . then, a=2 . the letter A is used twise in the word Kaplan and thus is represented by the
       number 125627 so the word karluk   must be equal to, 128691 ..   l+u+k=6+9+1=16

88.   If   kukak,kula,kevin→15678,1243,12131 then   v+i+n=?
       a)18 b)19   c)20   d)21   e)22

answer:d

       solution: as the first and the last letters of the word kukak are the same, they represents 12131 . the
       word kula has   four letters and represents 1243 the number. the word kevin represents the number
       15678 .   v+i+n=6+7+8=21

89.   If   lake,lakes,lamar→12627,1234,12345   then   (a+k).(l+s)=?
        a)24   b)28   c)30   d)35   e)34

answer:d

solution: the first letters of   the word lake and lakes   are the same. And thus   have two   number that are similar 1234 and
12345 . then, the word lake represents 1234 and the word lakes represents 12345 . so,the word lamar represents 12627 .
(a+k).(l+s)=(2+3).(1+6)=35

90.   If   lared, ,largo ,leeds→12376,123456,14458 then,   (s+d).(e+o)=?

        a)121   b)122   c)124   d)126   e)130

answer:e

solution. the word laredo consists of six letters , it is represented by   the   number 123456 . here
l=1,a=2 then, the word largo represents 12376.   the letters L and A EQUAL 1 AND 2
RESPECTIVELY AND   IS REPRESENTED BY THE   NUMBER 12376. Leeds is   represented
by 14458   . (s+d).(e+0)=(8+5).(4+6)=130

91.   If   lake,lakes,lamar,leeds→12345,1234,12627,14485   then lamar=?
        a)12345   b)1234   c)12627   d)144 85   e)12348

answer:c

solution. the second and the fourth letters of the   word lamar are the same. so, the representing number
must be 12627 .

92.   If   macon,magna,malta,marina→129052,12782,12652,12345 then,   what does magna=?
        a)129052   b)12782   c)12652   d)12345   e)12344

answer:c

solution. all the second letters of words are a , and it   is represented by 2 . the last letters of the three
word ends with a .   macon ends by   n . macon as number represented by 12345. here   n =5 . the word of
which the fourth number is five is   12652 .

93.   If napa ,nampa,newark,nema,wark→1232,12432,152678,1549,2678 then wark=?
        a)1232   b)12432   c)156278   d)1549   e)2678

answer:e

solution: the four words start with by the letter n . but the word wark start with w . so, the
representing number is 2678 .

94.   If oconto,ocala, omak, orem ,omar,→1907,1758,12565,121341 ,1759   then what does omar=?
        a)1907   b)1758   c)12565   d)121341   e)1759

answer:e

solution: the first three letters of omak and omar are the same. And are represented by the number
1758 and 1759 the word orem is represented by 1907   o=1,r=9,e=0
the word omar   ends in r thus   signifying the word   omar =1759

95..   If palmer,pampa,palatka,panama,papa→129242,1232782,12412,123456,1212   then what does palmer =?

a)129242 b)1232782 c)12412   d)123456 e)1212

answer:d

solution: the word palmer ends in r and the other four words end in a . the number 123456 represents the word palmer.

97.   If paris, parma,pasco, payson,paso→129580,12578,12362,12345,1258   then what does , payson=?

a)129580 b)12578 c)12362 d)12345 e)1258

answer:a

solution: the first three letters of paris ,parma ,pascoand paso are the same. they are represented by 12578,1258,12362 , 12345 . the word payson is equal to 129580

98.   If   pekin,peel,pella,penn,pen→1255,12667,1226,12345,125   then pekin=?

a)1255   b)12667 c)1226 d)12345 e)125

answer:d

solution: the word pen is represented by 125 . in the word peel,pella,penn first two the same two letters are written consecutively. these are represented by 1255,12667,1226 . the word pekin is represented by 12345.

99.   If rayen,rayne,redan,rolla,roll→18992,14725,12654,12345,1899   then rayne=?

a)18992   b)14725 c)12654   d)12345 e)1899

answer:12654

solution: the last letters of the two words are n and represented by rayen and redan 12725 and 12345 here n=5 oluyor. the fourth letter of rayne is n. the fourth letter is n and represented by 5 is 12654 .

100.   If saco,sage,salem,selma,mall→16782,14725,13654,12345,8277   then selma =?

a)1234 b)1256   c)12768 d)16782 e)8277

answer:a

solution: the second letter of the four words is a. the second letter of selma is e . and is represented by number 16782 .

101.   If   ada,ajo,bly,day→217,567,134,121 then, d+a+y=?

a)10 b)12 c)13 d)14 e)15

answer.a

solution. the word ada is represented by 121 . if a=1,d=2 then ,the word day is represented by 217. d+a+y=2+1+7=10

102.   If   waco,wall,ware, wood→1234,1255,1262,1889   then l+o=?

a)11   b)12   c)13 d)14 e)15

answer:13

solution: the last two letters of the word wall are the same it is represented by 1255 . the second and the third letters of the word wood are the same and it is represented by 1889. l+o=5+8=13

103.	If	page,pana, peel, peru → 1234,1252,1446,1478	then	n+e=?
a)9	b)10	c)11	d)12	e)13

answer:a

solution: as the third and the fourth letters are the same, the word pana is represented by 1252 . so, n=5, as the second and the third letters are the same, the word peel is represented by 1446.
e=4, n+e=4+5

104.	If	ada,adak,adin,ames→121,1213,1245,1678	then	k+n+s=?
a)12	b) 13 c) 14	d) 15	e)16

answer:16

solution: the ada is represented by 121 . the word adak is represented by 1213 thus , a=1,d=2 ,k=3 in the word adin is represented by 1245 and the word ames is represented by 1678 .
k+n+s=3+5+8=16

105.	If	baker,basin,bear,bison→17698,1425;12678;12345	then	bison =?

a)17698	b)12678	c)1425	d)12345	e)1236

answer:a

solution: the last letters of the word end in n. the words basin and bison are represented by 12678 and 17698. the first two letters of baker and basin words are the same and represented by 12345 and 12678 . if a=2 then ,basin=12678 and bison=17698 .

Quiz 1

1. if   all,fall,fill,call,cell→5622,122,3122,3422,5122   then   fill=?

    a)122   b)3122   c)3422   d)5122   e)5622

2. if   add,arm,art,age,bad→122,812,134,135,167   then   age=?

    a)122   b)812   c)134   d)135   d)167

3. if   away,baby,body,book,ball→4188,4557,1213,4143,4563   then   l+w=?

    a)6   B)7   c)8   D)9   e)10

4. if   atlas,away,ball,bill,call→9133,12314,1516,7133,7833   then   t+w=?

    a)4   b)5   c)6   d)7   e)8

5. call,keen,tall,sell,cell→1533,8533,7233,4556,1233   if   n+c=?

    a)6   b)7   c)8   d)9   E)1O

6. if   dad,all,odd,mad,fan→411,121,233,521,627   then   n+l+d=?

    a)9   b)1O   c)11   d)12   e)13

7. if   fan,far,fax,few,f→184,123,124,125,167   then   (w+r).(f+r)=?

    a)33   b)3O   c)28   d)25   e)55

8. if   big,bit,can,car,raw→ 568,869,123,124,567   then   g+t=?

    a)3   b)4   c)5   d)6   e)7

9. if   boss,book,onto,fall,fool→7229,1233,1224,2562,7899   then   fall=?

    A)7229   b)1233   c)1224   d)2562   e)7899

10. if   good,feet,here,gene,feed→9505,4553,1223,4556,7585   then   feet=?

    a)9505   b) 4553   c)1223   d)4556   e)7585

11. if   boy,all,day,bar,raw→123,748,147,643,455   then (l+y)/b

a)3   b)5   c)7   d)8   e)9

12. if   fan,far,fat,fax,for →124,123,174,126,125 then   for=?

a)124   b)123   c)174   d)126   e)125

13. if   gale,game,gang,gene,give→1254,1234,1784,1464,1261 then (n+a+e+i)=?

a)18   b)19   c)20   d)21   e)23

14. if get, gig, kid,tax→141,123,546,378 then (k+t)/(a+e)

a)8/9   b)9/8   c)7/8   d)8/7   e)2

15. if   hand,hang,hard→1264,1234,1235   then r=?

a)6   b)5   c)4   d)3   e)2

16. if   here,hard,door→5663,1435,1232   then e+o=?

a)6   b)7   c)8   d)9   e)1O

17. if   keen,keep,kill→1223,1566,1224   then   n+p+i=?

a)12   B)13   c)14   d)15   e)16

18. if   fall,tall,pool→4233,1233,5663   then (a+o)/L

a)7/3   b)8/3   c)8/5   d)7/5   e)3

19. if   kill,miss,peep,pool→6883,1233,4255,6776   then (i+e+o)/L

a)19/4   b)19/3   c)17/3   d)17/4   e)3

2O.   if   pain,pale,pass,well→8655,1234,1256,1277   then (e+l)/s

a)11/7   b)11/4   c)11/5   d)12/7   e)3

Quiz 2

1. if   mad,man,dad,all,let→567,123,128,323,255 then (t+L+n+d)=?

    a)14   b)16   c)17   d)18   e)23

2. if   war,way,wet,tow→156,781,123,124 then (w+r+y)=?

    A)10   B)9   c)8   d)7   e)6

3. if pay,pop,put,tap→621,123,141,156 then pay+tap=?

    a)744 b)624 c)544 d)524   e)433

4. if sad,saw,set,see→155,123,124,156 then set+see=?

    a)211 b)223   c)266 d)311   e)411

5. if   peep,pool,prop→1531,1221,1334 then   peep+prop=?

    a)1752   b)1852   c)2252   d)2752   e)2802

6. if tall,talk,kill,keep→4533,4667,1233,1234   then talk+keep=?

    a)3902 b)4901 c)4901   d)5901   e)2901

7. if   war,wet,way→126,123,145 then   (t+e)/w

    a)7 b)8   c)9   d)10 E)11

8. if   law,lay,let,war→327,123,124,146 then   (e+t)/r

    a)6/5   b)7/6   c)8/7   d)10/7   e)11/9

9. if miss,sell,solo→3656,1233,3455 then   (o+s+L)=?

    a)11 b)12   c)13   d)14   e)15

10. if sent,solo,soon→1553,1234,1565 then (L+t).(o+s)=?

    a)50   B)55   c)60   d)66 e)77

11.   if   land,lane,last,look→1889,1234,1267,1235 then s+t+k=?

a)18   b)19 c)20   d)21   e)22

12.   if   near,need,neat,rear→4232,1234,1225,1236 then near+rear=?

a)5488 b)5466   c)4444 d)3488   e)5433

13.   if   rain,rare,rear,rest→1521,1567,1215,1234 then e*r=?

a)7   b)8   c)9 d)10   e)11

14.   if   mess,mist,mood,soon→3668,1233,1435,1667 then   e+s+i+t=?

a)11 b)12 c)13   d)14   e)15

15.   if   tale,talk,tall,tell→1433,1234,1235,1233 then   tall+tell=?

a)2622   b)2566   c)2666 d)2344 e)2455

16. if   sale, sell, solo,some,soon→1557,1234,1433,1535,1564 then   sale=?

a)1557   b)1234   c)1433   d)1535   e)1564

17.   if like,line,list,look→1883,1267,1234,1254 then e+k=?

a)4 b)5 c)6 d)7   e)8

18.   if fool, fill, free,full→1733,1223,1433,1566   then   fool+free=?

a)2388 b)3288 c)2566 d)2787 e)2789

19.   if   odd,off,old,sob→142,516,122,133 then   old+sob=?

a)658 b)558   c)458 d)444 e0543

20.   if hand,hang, game, gate→5287,1234,1235,5267   then h+a+n+d=?

a)11 b)10 c)9 d)8 e)7

Quiz 3

1. if less,like,list,look→1775,1233,1452,1436   then less+look=?

    a)3003 b)4005 c)3008 d)4444 e)3333

2. if   logo,long,lost,solo→5212,1232,1243,1256 then long+lost=?

    a)2188 b)3211 c)2188 d)2499 e)2199

3. if   make,meet,game,gave→6274,1234,1445,6214 t h e n take=?

    a)6274 b)1234 c)1445 d)6214 e)5234

4. if   need,mood,mist, sell→7299,1223,4553,4678 then solo=?

    a)7595 b)7696 c)4565 d)5656 e)4575

5. if   miss,mood,mild→1265,1233,1445 then   solo=?

    a)3464 b)4353 c)2353 d)5656 e)2434

6. if   warn,warm,wood→1667,1234,1235   then   madam=?

    a)52824 b)62725 c)42625 d)32725 e052725

7. if   pain,pale,pas→1277,1234,1256   then   sale=?

    a)7256 b)6256 c)4356 d)3256 e)2346

8. if   long,look,lost→1267,1234,1225 then k+l+o=?

    a)8 b)9 c)10 d)11 e)12

9. if rob,run,raw,war→761,123,145,167 then raw+war=?

    a)528 b)628 c)728 d)828 e)928

10. if   line,link,late,list→1287,1234,1235,1674 t h e n   e+t+a+l=?

a)17 b)18 c)19 d)20 e)21

11. if   apart,award,away,atlas→14819,12134,15136,1517, then atlas=?

a)14819 b)12134 c)15136 d)1517 e)12164

12. if   away,atlas,ball→7155,1213,14516   then y+t+b=?

a)11 b)12   c)13 d)14 e)15

13. if   can,car,cup,mad,raw→156,728,429,123,124   then   cup+mad=?

a)584 b)684 c)784 d)884 e)1157

14. if   way,wet,tow,top,map→827,123,145,561,527,   then tap+map=?

a)1154 b)1254   c)1354 d)1464 e)2424

15. if   last,land,data,call→7211,1234,1256,6242   then   land+data=?

a)2489 b)5488 c)6544 d)7498 e)8654

16. if   pale,pain,pant,pass,sent→ 8467,1234,1256,1267,1288   then sent+pass=?

a)9755 b)8755 c)7755 d)6755 e)5656

17. if   take,talk,meet,kill→3755,1234,1253,6441 t h e n   k+l+a+t=?

a)6 b)7 c)8 d)10 e)11

18. if   book,bore,boss,solo→6272,1223,1245,1266   then o+r+s+l=/

a)15 b)17 c)19 d)20 e)21

19. if   hum,how,hot,hit→176,123,145,146 then   hum+hit=?

a)134 b299 c)300 d)311   e)333

20. if   hard,hate,hang,hand→1234,1274,1278,1256 t h e n   n+a=?

a)6 b)7 c)8 d)9 e)10

Quia 4

1. if   keen,tall,meet,tool→4886,1223,4566,7224   then   n+l+t=?

    a)13 b)12 c)11 d)10 e)9

2. if   act,age,all,art→173,123,145,166   then   age+all=?

    a)111 b)211   c)222 d)311 e)411

3. if   face,fact,fame,fell→1264,1477,1234,1235   then   e+c+a+f+=?

    a)7 b)8 c)9 d)10 e)11

4. if   map,mud,dad,all→145,123,565,677   then   l+a=?

    a)10 b)11 c)12 d)13 e)14

5. if   fold,fill,free, fame→1897,1234,1533,1677   then   fame-fold=?

    a)663 b)653 c)764 d)544 e)732

6. if   pray,press,prop,pure→1825,1271,12566,1234   then   pure-pray=?

    a)591 b)588 c)544 d)688 e)611

7. if   fill,fold,fool,free→1443,1688,1233,1435   then fool-fold=?

    a)11 b)10 c)9 d)8 e)7

8. if   lamb,lamp,lane,last→1234,1289,1267,1235   then lamp-lamb=?

    a)6 b)5 c)4 d)3 e)1

9. if   gene,game,gate,give→1782,1232,1452,1462   then   give-gene=?

    a)650 b)550 c)450 d)350 e)250

10. if   mind,mild,miss,mist→1267,1234,1254,1266   then   mist-miss=?

    a)1 b)2 c)3 d)4 e)5

11. if motor,press,sleet,atlas→93897,12324,54677,78663   then sleet-press=?

a)23117 b)23422 c)23111 d)24112 e)023986

12. if   fold,fool,data,door→4227,1234,1223,4565 t h e n   data-fold=?

a)1111 b)2222 c)3333 d)3331 e)2221

13. if away,ball,fall,tall→7155,1213,4155,6155 t h e n   y+w+l=?

a)6 b)7 c)8 d)9 e)10

14. if   warm,well,wood,tool→1778,9776,1234,1566   then o+l+m=?

a)16 b)17 c)18 d)19 e)20

15. if   rain,rare,rest,rise→1567,1365,1234,1215 then   rest-rise=?

a)102 b)109 c)200 d)202 e)222

16. if off,old,sob,boy→516,617,122,134   then boy-sob=?

a)100 b)101 c0103 d)105 e)122

17. if   near,neat, need, meet→1226,7225,1235,1234   t h e n   neat-near=?

a)6 b)5 c)4 d)3 e)1

18. if deep,door, dull,data,tall→1445,1223,1677,1898,9877 then a+t+d=?

a)17 b)18 c)19 d)20 e)21

19. if make,mess,mild,mist→1455,1234,1678,1659 then   mess-make=?

a)111 b)121 c)222 d)221 e)232

20. if cell,come, cure,card→1452,1233,1672,1879 t h e n   card-cell=?

a)346 b)445 c)546 d)646 e)54

Operations and natural numbers

1. $\dfrac{\triangle \; \triangle \; \triangle}{\triangle} + 44 = \odot \boxdot \boxdot$ and $\boxdot \odot = ?$

A) 41   B) 51   C) 61   D) 71   E) 72

Explanation:

$\triangle = 2$ if,

$\dfrac{222}{2} + 44 = 111 + 44 = 155 = \odot \boxdot \boxdot$ if the,

$\odot = 1, \boxdot = 5$ one can. Then, $\boxdot \odot = 51$ **answer: B**

2.   AB and find the bigger volue of the ABC.
   BC
  $+$CA
  ‾‾‾‾
   176

A) 861   B) 961   C) 671   D) 972   E) 762

Explanation: AB $\rightarrow$ 10A + B
            BC $\rightarrow$ 10B + C
           $+$CA $\rightarrow$ 10C + A
           ‾‾‾‾‾‾‾‾‾‾‾
            176 $= 11(A + B + C)$
            A + B + C = 16

A = 9, B = 6, C = 1 to yield.   **answer: B**

3.
$$\begin{array}{r} 12A \\ \times\, BA \\ \hline - \ - \ - \\ -\ -4 \\ +\ \\ \hline 4 \end{array}$$

$A \times B = ?$

A) 12   B) 16   C) 17   D) 24   E) 27

Explanation:
$A \cdot A = 8 \cdot 8 = 64$ if,
$128 \cdot B8 = \ldots 4$ can write.
last digit of the multiple ab is 4.

$$\begin{array}{r} 128 \\ \times\ 38 \\ \hline 1024 \\ +384 \\ \hline 4864 \end{array}$$

if the, $A = 8$, $B = 3$ be. $A \cdot B = 24$

answer: D

4.
$$\begin{array}{r} ab \\ aa \qquad ca \\ +bb \qquad +bc \\ \hline 165 \quad\ 187 \end{array}$$
and
$$\begin{array}{r} cc \\ +ab \\ \hline ?? \end{array}$$

A) 109   B) 108   C) 100   D) 106   E) 105

Explanation:
$$\begin{array}{r} aa \\ +bb \\ \hline 165 \end{array}$$
and

$aa \rightarrow 11a$
$bb \rightarrow 11b$
$aa + bb = 11(a + b)$
$\qquad 165 = 11(a + b)$
$\qquad\quad a + b = 15$

$a = 7$, $b = 8$ given that,
$$\begin{array}{r} 78 \\ c7 \\ +8c \\ \hline 187 \end{array}$$
one can.

As can be seen $c = 2$. Then
$$\begin{array}{r} 22 \\ +78 \\ \hline 100 \end{array}$$
be.

answer: C

5.
$$\begin{array}{r} AB \\ +BB \\ \hline 58 \end{array} \quad \begin{array}{r} CB \\ +AD \\ \hline 101 \end{array} \quad \text{and } C \quad ?$$

A) 5   B) 6   C) 7   D) 8   E) 9

Explanation: $B + B = 8$ $A + B = 5$
$2B = 8$ $A + 4 = 5$
$B = 4$ $A = 1$
$B + D = 11$ $C + A = 9$
$4 + D = 11$ $C + 1 = 9$
$D = 7$ $C = 8$

answer: D

6.
$$\begin{array}{r} aa \\ bb \\ +cc \\ \hline 66 \end{array} \quad \begin{array}{r} bb \\ +aa \\ \hline cc \end{array} \quad \text{and } c = ?$$

A) 3   B) 4   C) 5   D) 6   E) 7

Explanation: $a + b + c = 6$ $b + a = c$
$c + c = 6$
$2c = 6$
$c = 3$

answer: A

7.
$$\begin{array}{r} abb \\ + aa \\ \hline 765 \end{array} \quad \text{if } 2a - b = ?$$

A) 3   B) 4   C) 5   D) 6   E) 7

Explanation: $a + b = 15$
$a = 6, b = 9$ given that,
$$\begin{array}{r} 699 \\ + 66 \\ \hline 765 \end{array} \quad \text{one can. } 2a - b = 2 \cdot 6 - 9 = 3$$

answer: A

8. $\quad$ a2b $\quad$ a + b = ?
    $\quad$ x $\underline{\quad 11 \quad}$
    $\quad\quad$ . . .
    $\quad$ + $\underline{\quad . . . \quad}$
    $\quad\quad$ 576b

A) 6 $\quad\quad$ B) 7 $\quad\quad$ C) 8 $\quad\quad$ D) 9 $\quad\quad$ E) 10

Explanation: $\quad$ a2b $\quad\quad$ b + 2 = 6
$\quad\quad\quad\quad\quad$ x $\underline{\quad 11 \quad}$
$\quad\quad\quad\quad\quad\quad$ a 2 b
$\quad\quad\quad\quad$ + $\underline{\text{a 2 b}}$
$\quad\quad\quad\quad\quad$ 576b
$\quad\quad\quad\quad$ b = 4
$\quad\quad\quad\quad$ a + 2 = 7
$\quad\quad\quad\quad$ a = 5
$\quad\quad\quad\quad$ a + b = 5 + 4 = 9

answer: D

Tables

1.

6	10	8	6
10	12	3	5
5	6	3	16
3	4	5	x

x = ?

A) 12 $\quad\quad$ B) 15 $\quad\quad$ C) 16 $\quad\quad$ D) 18 $\quad\quad$ E) 20

Explanation: the some of the given numbers left the right should be 30.
6 + 8 + 10 + 6 = 30
10 + 12 + 3 + 5 = 30,
3 + 4 + 5 + x = 30 → x = 18

answer: D

2.

6	4	5
10	8	9
9	11	10
6	20	x

x = ?

A) 10   B) 11   C) 12   D) 13   E) 15

Explanation:

a	b	c

In every row of the table half of the sum of the number is first two column.

$$c = \frac{a+b}{2}, \quad x = \frac{6+20}{2} \Rightarrow x = 13$$

answer: D

3.

20	1	3
15	2	2
12	1	5
30	2	x

x = ?

A) 5   B) 4   C) 3   D) 2   E) 1

Explanation:

a	b	c

the preduct of the number is any row of the table is equal to 60.

$a \cdot b \cdot c = 60$

$30 \cdot 2 \cdot x = 60$

$x = 1$

answer: E

4.

3	4	5
5	12	13
8	15	17
10	24	x

$x = ?$

A) 26   B) 28   C) 30   D) 32   E) 34

Explanation:

a	b	c

All any row of the table sum of the squares of the number in first two columns is equal to the sequar of the number in third column.

$a^2 + b^2 = c^2$
$3^2 + 4^2 = 25 = 5^2$
$5^2 + 12^2 = 169 = 13^2$
$8^2 + 15^2 = 289 = 17^2$
$10^2 + 24^2 = x^2$
$x = 26$

answer:A

5.

+	A	B	C
A		14	
B			18
C	16		

$A \cdot B \cdot C = ?$

A) 460   B) 480   C) 470   D) 440   E) 430

Explanation:

$A + B = 14$
$B + C = 18$
$A + C = 16$
$+$
_____
$2(A + B + C) = 48$
$A + B + C = 24$

$A \cdot B \cdot C = 480$

$A + B + C = 24$
$14 + C = 24$
$\boxed{C = 10}$
$B + C = 18$
$B + 10 = 18$
$\boxed{B = 8}$
$A + B = 14$
$A + 8 = 14$
$\boxed{A = 6}$

answer:B

6.

α	↓	↑	→
⊙	△	↑	⊙
→	□	✱	△
□	?	↓	α

Which figure should be in place of the guestion mark?

A) α   B) ↓   C) ⊙   D) □   E) ✱

Explanation:
There should be two copies of every figure and we have one star . the ather stars should be in place of guestion mark.

answer: E

7.

X	a	b	c
a		48	
b			24
c	18		

A) 18   B) 17   C) 16   D) 15   E) 14

Explanation:

$$a \cdot b = 48$$
$$b \cdot c = 24$$
$$c \cdot a = 18$$
$$\overline{a^2 \cdot b^2 \cdot c^2 = 48 \cdot 24 \cdot 18}$$
$$a \cdot b \cdot c = 144$$

$a \cdot b = 48$ $a \cdot b \cdot c = 144$
$48 \cdot c = 144$
$c = 3$

$b \cdot c = 24$ $a \cdot b = 48$
$b \cdot 3 = 24$ $a \cdot 8 = 48$
$b = 8$ $a = 6$

$a + b + c = 6 + 8 + 3 = 17$

answer: B

Operations

1. $3 \blacktriangle 1 = 10$ Which number should be in place of the guestion mark?
    $4 \blacktriangle 2 = 20$
    $5 \blacktriangle 3 = 34$
    $6 \blacktriangle 4 = ?$
    A) 42   B) 52   C) 54   D) 57   E) 62
    Explanation:
    $a \blacktriangle b \rightarrow c$
    $c = a^2 + b^2$
    $6 \blacktriangle 4 \rightarrow c$
    $c = 6^2 + 4^2$
    $c = 52$

    answer: B

2. $24 \square 32 \rightarrow 86$
    $42 \square 14 \rightarrow 84$
    $13 \square 22 \rightarrow 34$
    $71 \square 42 \rightarrow ?$
    Which number should be in place of the guestion mark?
    A) 76   B) 77   C) 78   D) 79   E) 80

    Explanation:
    $ab \square cd \rightarrow mn$
    $a \cdot b = m; \ c \cdot d = n \Rightarrow m = 7 \cdot 1 = 7;$
    $n = 4 \cdot 2 = 8$
    $71 \square 42 \rightarrow 78$

    answer: C

3. $3 \odot 4 \rightarrow 13$
    $4 \odot 6 \rightarrow 32$
    $2 \odot 5 \rightarrow 23$
    $3 \odot 7 \rightarrow ?$
    Which number should be in place of the guestion mark?
    A) 46   B) 45   C) 44   D) 43   E) 42

    Explanation:
    $a \odot b \rightarrow c$
    $c = b^2 - a$
    $3 \odot 7 \rightarrow 7^2 - 3 = 49 - 3 = 46$
    $3 \odot 7 \rightarrow 46$

    answer: A

4. $6 \boxplus 4 \to 5$

$7 \boxplus 2 \to \dfrac{9}{5}$

$8 \boxplus 4 \to 3$

$9 \boxplus 3 \to ?$

Which figure should be in place of the guestion mark?
A) 2   B) 3   C) 4   D) 5   E) 6

Explanation:

$a \boxplus b \to c$

$c = \dfrac{a + b}{a - b}$

$9 \boxplus 3 \to c \qquad c = \dfrac{9 + 3}{9 - 3} = \dfrac{12}{6} = 2$

answer: A

5. $(3 * 2) \blacktriangle 4 \to 5$

$(6 * 4) \blacktriangle 3 \to 5$

$(7 * 6) \blacktriangle 9 \to 10$

$(8 * 5) \blacktriangle 5 \to ?$

Which figure should be in place of the guestion mark?
A) 9   B) 10   C) 5   D) 6   E) 8

Explanation:

$(a * b) \blacktriangle c \to m$
$m = (a - b) + c$
$m = (8 - 5) + 5$
$m = 3 + 5$
$m = 8$

answer: E

6. $8 \bullet 7 \to 1$

$9 \bullet 6 \to 27$

$14 \bullet 10 \to 64$

$15 \bullet 10 \to ?$

Which figure should be in place of the guestion mark?
A) 25   B) 75   C) 100   D) 125   E) 135

Explanation:

$a \bullet b \to c$
$c = (a - b)^3$
$c = (15 - 10)^3$
$c = 125$

answer: D

7. $8 \boxdot 4 \rightarrow \dfrac{1}{3}$

$6 \boxdot 2 \rightarrow \dfrac{1}{2}$

$12 \boxdot 3 \rightarrow \dfrac{3}{5}$

$16 \boxdot 8 \rightarrow ?$

Which number should be in place of the question mark?

A) $\dfrac{1}{3}$ B) $\dfrac{1}{2}$ C) $\dfrac{1}{4}$ D) $\dfrac{1}{5}$ D) $\dfrac{1}{6}$

Explanation:

$a \boxdot b \rightarrow \dfrac{a-b}{a+b}$

$16 \boxdot 8 \rightarrow \dfrac{16-8}{16+8} = \dfrac{8}{24} = \dfrac{1}{3}$

answer: A

8. $8 \triangle 4 \rightarrow 12, 4, 32$

$9 \triangle 3 \rightarrow 12, 6, 27$

$5 \triangle 1 \rightarrow 6, 4, 5$

$9 \triangle 5 \rightarrow ?, ?, ?$

Choose the correct answer.

A) $13, 3, 44$ B) $14, 4, 40$ C) $14, 4, 45$ D) $45, 4, 14$ E) $14, 4, 44$

Explanation:

$a \triangle b = (a+b); (a-b); (a \cdot b)$

$9 \triangle 5 \rightarrow 14, 4, 45$

answer: C

9. $9 \odot 4 \rightarrow 24$

$8 \odot 6 \rightarrow 35$

$4 \odot 5 \rightarrow 12$

$7 \odot 6 \rightarrow ?$

Which number should be in place of the question mark?

A) 24 B) 25 C) 28 D) 27 E) 30

Explanation:

$a \odot b \rightarrow (a-1) \cdot (b-1)$

$7 \odot 6 \rightarrow (7-1) \cdot (6-1) = 6 \cdot 5 = 30$

$7 \odot 6 \rightarrow 30$

answer: E

10. $64 \square 5 \rightarrow 15$
    $72 \square 3 \rightarrow 12$
    $54 \square 6 \rightarrow 15$
    $48 \square 2 \rightarrow ?$
    Which number should be in place of the question mark?
    A) 14   B) 13   C) 12   D) 11   E) 9

    Explanation:
    $ab \square c \rightarrow m$
    $m = (a + b + c)$
    $48 \square 2 \rightarrow m = (4 + 8 + 2) = 14$

    answer: A

Whats the relationship between number and figures?

1.

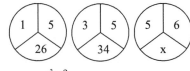

$x^2 = ?$

A) 60   B) 61   C) 51   D) 30   E) 65

Explanation:

$a^2 + b^2 = c^2$
$5^2 + 6^2 = x^2$
$x^2 = 61$

answer: B

2.

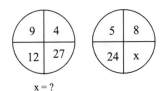

$x = ?$

A) 10   B) 12   C) 14   D) 15   E) 16

Explanation:

$x = 5 \cdot 3$
$x = 15$

answer: D

3.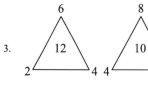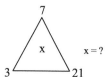

A) 48   B) 49   C) 28   D) 27   E) 30

Explanation: 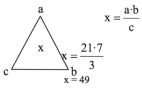 $x = \dfrac{a \cdot b}{c}$

$x = \dfrac{21 \cdot 7}{3}$

$x = 49$

answer: B

4.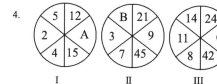

I   II   III

$A + B + C = ?$

A) 54   B) 64   C) 74   D) 68   E) 72

Explanation:

$A = 3 \cdot 2$
$A = 6$
$45 = 3b$
$B = 15$
$C = 3 \cdot 11$
$C = 33$

$A + B + C = 6 + 15 + 33 = 54$

answer: A

5.

I

4	5	7
12	15	A

II

9	10	20
6	7	B

III

10	14	C
5	7	24

$A + B + C = ?$

A) 66   B) 67   C) 76   D) 78   E) 86

Explanation: 1.

a	b	c
3a	3b	3c

2.

a	b	c
a − 3	b − 3	c − 3

3.

2a	2b	2c
a	b	c

$A = 3a = 3 \cdot 7 = 21$
$B = 20 - 3 = 17$
$C = 2C = 2 \cdot 24 = 48$
$A + B + C = 21 + 17 + 48 = 86$
$A + B + C = 86$

answer: E

6.

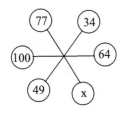

$x = ?$

A) 186   B) 196   C) 206   D) 216   E) 236

Explanation:

$x = (a + b)^2$
$x = (7 + 7)^2$
$x = 196$

answer: B

7.

| 87 |——| 62 | 52 | x = ?

| 98 |——| 36 | 26 |

| x |——| 24 | 32 |

A) 64   B) 65   C) 74   D) 75   E) 80

Explanation:

| ab |——| xy | mn |

$a \rightarrow x + y, b = m + n$
$x \rightarrow ab$
$a \rightarrow (2 + 4) = 6, b = (3 + 2) = 5$
$x \rightarrow 65$

answer: B

8.

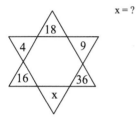

x = ?

A) 10   B) 12   C) 8   D) 18   E) 22

Explanation:
Multiple of same number comes up to 144, what numbers are they.
$16 \cdot 9 = 144, \ 36 \cdot 4 = 144,$
$x \cdot 18 = 144$
$x = 8$

answer: C

9.

x + y = ?

A) 22   B) 23   C) 24   D) 25   E) 27

Explanation:

$x = a + b$
$y = (a + b) - 1$
$x = 5 + 9 = 14$
$y = 5 + 9 - 1 = 13$
$x + y = 27$

answer: E

10.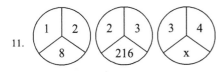

A) 12   B) 13   C) 31   D) 21   E) 26

Explanation:

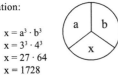

$x = (a + b) = mn \rightarrow nm$
$x = (8 + 4) = 12 \rightarrow 21$

answer: D

11.

$x = ?$

A) 1628   B) 1728   C) 1682   D) 1528   E) 1425

Explanation:

$x = a^3 \cdot b^3$
$x = 3^3 \cdot 4^3$
$x = 27 \cdot 64$
$x = 1728$

answer: B

12. 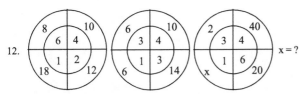 $x = ?$

A) 10   B) 11   C) 15   D) 20   E) 24

Explanation:

$a \cdot b \cdot c \cdot d = x + y + m + n$
$3 \cdot 4 \cdot 6 \cdot 1 = x + 40 + 20 + 2$
$72 = x + 62$
$x = 10$

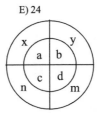

answer: A

13.

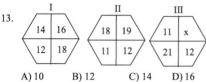

A) 10   B) 12   C) 14   D) 16   E) 18

Explanation:

$a + b + c + d = 60$
$11 + 21 + 12 + x = 60$
$x = 16$

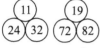

answer: D

14.

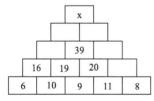

$x = ?$

A) 12   B) 16   C) 18   D) 19   E) 20

Explanation:
$x = a + b + c + d$
$x = 4 + 4 + 8 + 4$
$x = 20$

answer: E

15.

A) 140   B) 142   C) 150   D) 152   E) 168

Explanation:

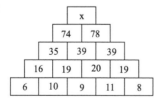

$x = 74 + 78$
$x = 152$

answer: D

16.

A) 20   B) 21   C) 22   D) 23   E) 24

Explanation:

$x = a + b + c + m + n + z$
$x = 2 + 2 + 2 + 6 + 6 + 6$
$x = 24$

answer: E

17.

$x = ?$

A) 10   B) 11   C) 12   D) 13   E) 14

Explanation: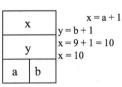

$x = a + 1$
$y = b + 1$
$x = 9 + 1 = 10$
$x = 10$

answer: A

18.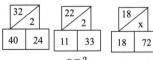

$x = ?$

A) 1   B) 9   C) 3   D) 5   E) 6

Explanation: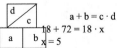

$a + b = c \cdot d$
$18 + 72 = 18 \cdot x$
$x = 5$

answer: D

19. 4 → 324, ([4] 3) → 4053
                                      [5]

    ([2] 6) → ?
    ([8] [7])

A) 1700   B) 1776   C) 1076   D) 1066   E) 1476

Explanation: □ = 10, ⬜ = 100

$\boxed{2}$ = 2 · 10 · 10 = 200

$\boxed{8}$ = 8 · 10 · 10 = 800

$\boxed{7}$ = 7 · 10 = 70

Cəmi = 200 + 700 + 70 + 6 = 1076
Cəmi = 1076

answer: C

20. (12) (24)(20) (29)(33) (31)   x = ?
       (6)   (7)   (x)

A) 8   B) 9   C) 10   D) 11   E) 12

Explanation: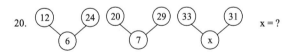

$x = \sqrt{a+b}$
$x = \sqrt{31+33}$
$x = \sqrt{64}$
$x = 8$

answer: A

21.

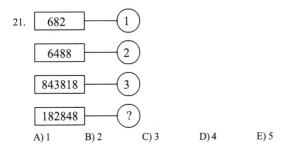

A) 1   B) 2   C) 3   D) 4   E) 5

Explanation:

answer: C

Find the relationship between two figures

1.

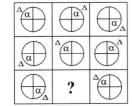

Which figure should be in place of the   guestion mark?

A)   B)   C)

D)   E)

Explanation: Delta and alpha figures moves toward clock wise.

answer: E

2.

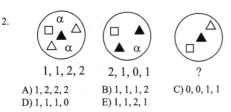

1, 1, 2, 2   2, 1, 0, 1   ?

A) 1, 2, 2, 2   B) 1, 1, 1, 2   C) 0, 0, 1, 1
D) 1, 1, 1, 0   E) 1, 1, 2, 1

Explanation:
Numbers on the figures will be written outside of the area. On the third area one of the three
figure is number.   **answer: D**

3.

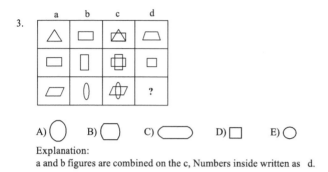

A) ◯   B) ⬭   C) ⬭   D) ☐   E) ◯

Explanation:
a and b figures are combined on the c, Numbers inside written as d.

answer: B

4.

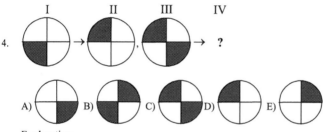

A)   B)   C)   D)   E)

Explanation:
First figure is throw to the right side with 90 degrees that will be your Second figure. When third figure throw to the right side with 90 degrees it will give you variant B.

answer: B

5.

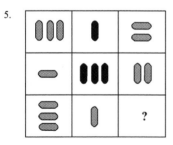

Which figure should be in place of the guestion mark?

A) ⬭   B) 🬀   C) 🬀   D) ◖◗   E) ❚❚

Explanation:
There should be three number from each figure. One of those figures needs to be black, missed figure is in variant E.

answer: E

I   II   III

6. → , → ?

Which figure should be in place of the guestion mark?

A)   B)   C)

D)   E)

Explanation: Ø △
When sides numbers decrees, Ø figures increase. Because of that, beside square if you get delta, Ø it will be 4.

answer: D

7.
A)   B)   C)

D)   E)

Explanation:

answer: D

8.

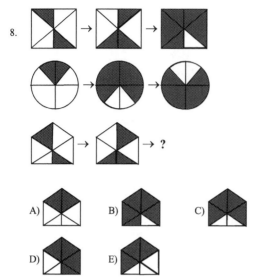

A)   B)   C)

D)   E)

Explanation:
When you put figure one and two top of each other, the parts intersect become white, other sides become black.

answer: B

9.

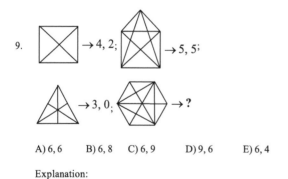

A) 6, 6   B) 6, 8   C) 6, 9   D) 9, 6   E) 6, 4

Explanation:

→ a, b

a - Define the number on the side of figures.
b- Define diagonal number on the figures.

→ 6 , 6 .

answer: A

10. → 5, 4; ⊞⊞ → 7, 6;

⊠ → 6, 4; ⬡ → ?

A) 6, 4   B) 6, 5   C) 5, 6   D) 6, 9   E) 9, 6

Explanation:

△ → a, b

a- How many line are there on figure?
b- Find out how many parts in the figure?

⬡ → 9 , 6

answer: E

TEST 1

1. Find the different number.
    A) 24   B) 27   C) 21   D) 34   E) 29

2. Find the different number.
    A) 400   B) 289   C) 225   D) 122   E) 196

3. Find the different number.
    A) 8   B) 27   C) 60   D) 64   E) 343

4. 64   84   92   81
    2   4   7   ?
    A) 7   B) 6   C) 5   D) 4   E) 2

5. 12   34   11   66
    5   25   2   ?

    A) 70   B) 72   C) 36   D) 48   E) 50

6. 7, 5, 15, 13, 39, 37, ?
    A) 111   B) 112   C) 113   D) 114   E) 115

7. 23, 29, 31, 37, ?
    A) 40   B) 42   C) 41   D) 43   E) 47

8. 12, 22, 23, 33, 43, ?
    A) 26   B) 24   C) 72   D) 29   E) 45

9. 2   4   3
    8   3   1
    12   2   1

    $\dfrac{1}{2}$ 3   x
    A) 30   B) 16   C) 34   D) 36   E) 40

10. 6   12   8
    10   12   4
    13   4   9
    18   2   x
    A) 3   B) 4   C) 6   D) 7   E) 8

11. $(3\triangle 4)\square 5 \rightarrow 20$
    $(2\triangle 3)\square 4 \rightarrow 9$
    $(7\triangle 1)\square 25 \rightarrow 25$
    $(8\triangle 4)\square 10 \rightarrow ?$

    A) 60   B) 65   C) 70   D) 75   E) 80

12. $64\square 22 \rightarrow 6$
    $79\square 15 \rightarrow 10$
    $84\square 62 \rightarrow 4$
    $99\square 18 \rightarrow ?$

    A) 9   B) 8   C) 7   D) 6   E) 5

13. $34\square \rightarrow 12; 7$
    $68\square \rightarrow 48; 14$
    $22\square \rightarrow 4; 4$
    $66\square \rightarrow ? ?$

    A) 36; 24   B) 36; 12   C) 36; 18   D) 12; 36   E) 36; 25

14. 10, 21, 32, 25, 72, ?
    A) 44   B) 45   C) 91   D) 79   E) 74

15. $(2\square 1)\triangle(8*2) \rightarrow 12$
    $(6\square 4)\triangle(9*3) \rightarrow 30$
    $(14\square 7)\triangle(2*7) \rightarrow 6$
    $(30\square 6)\triangle(2*3) \rightarrow ?$

    A) 20   B) 22   C) 24   D) 28   E) 30

16.   x = ?

    A) 30   B) 33   C) 34   D) 36   E) 40

17.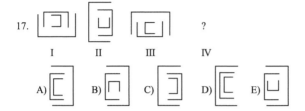

18.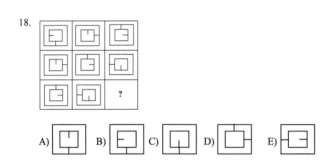

19.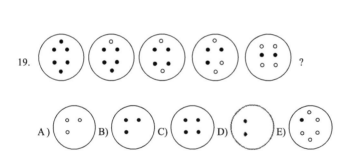

20.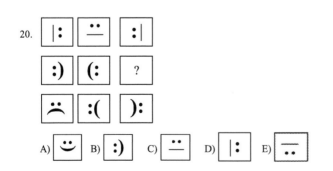

TEST 2

1.

▲ ○	▲ ✳	△ ✳
△ ✳	▲ ✳	?
▲ ✳	△ ○	▲ ✳

A) ▲ ○ B) ▲ ✳ C) ▲ ● D) ▲ ▲ E) ✳ ○

2.

△△△ △△△ △△△	△△△ △△△	△△△
△△ △△ △△	△△ △△	?
△ △ △	△ △	△

A) △△ △△ B) △△△ △△△ △△△ C) △△ D) △△△ △△△ E) △ △

3.

○ ●	● ●	● ○
● ○	○ ●	?
● ○	● ○	○ ●

A) ● ● B) ● ○ C) ○ ● D) ○ ● E) ○ ○

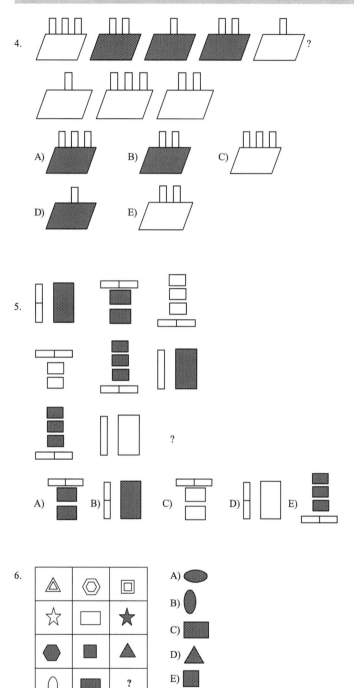

7.

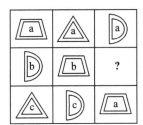

A) c   B) a   C) a   D) c   E) b

8.

*	▭	⬡	△
⬠	9	11	16
△	?	27	0

A) 7   B) 8   C) 12   D) 24   E) 21

9.

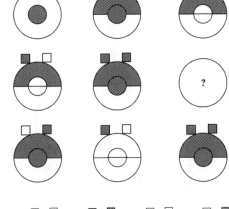

A)   B)   C)   D)   E)

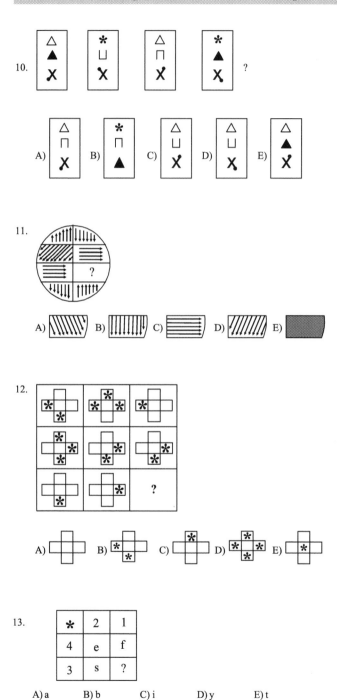

14.

*	2	3
18	A	S
12	S	?

A) A   B) İ   C) D   D) Ü   E) S

15.

*	4	5
1	F	S
3	S	?

A) S   B) Y   C) D   D) Ü   E) İ

16. 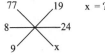 x = ?

A) 8   B) 9   C) 10   D) 11   E) 6

17. x = ?

A) 18   B) 20   C) 24   D) 30   E) 36

18.
```
77      19      x = ?
8 ---X--- 24
9      x
```

A) 14   B) 28   C) 49   D) 59   E) 73

19.
```
88      14      x = ?
72 ---X--- 9
5      x
```

A) 12   B) 15   C) 14   D) 16   E) 17

20.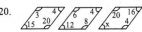

A) 5   B) 6   C) 7   D) 8   E) 10

TEST 3

1.

6	10
8	12

8	20
4	16

8	2
x	4

   A) 7   B) 8   C) 9   D) 10   E) 12

2.

Circle I: 4 | 5 / 1 | 3
Circle II: 16 | 25 / 1 | 9
Circle III: 7 | 12 / 17 | 14
IV: ?

    I   II   III   IV

A) 49 | 144 / 280 | 196   B) 49 | 142 / 289 | 196   C) 49 | 144 / 289 | 196   D) 49 | 140 / 279 | 186   E) 14 | 24 / 34 | 28

3.

Triangle 1: 3 / 8 1
Triangle 2: 12 / 2 1
Triangle 3: 48 / 1 x

   A) 1   B) 2   C) $\dfrac{1}{2}$ D) $\dfrac{1}{3}$ E) $\dfrac{1}{4}$

4.

Triangle 1: 3 / 5 4
Triangle 2: 5 / 12 13
Triangle 3: x / 40 9

   A) 7   B) 6   C) 5   D) 8   E) 9

5.

abc	c	ab
cba	b	ca
mnc	m	x

   A) nm   B) mn   C) nmc   D) nc   E) cmn

6.

abc	ab	bc
mnc	mc	nc
mnk	mn	x

A) mk   B) kn   C) mnk   D) mk   E) nk

7.

7	10	12
15	12	2
16	13	x

A) 1   B) 2   C) 3   D) 0   E) 4

8.

ab   bc   ?

A) aabc   B) abca   C) abba   D) abbc   E) cbba

9.

aaa   aaaa   ?

A) aaabb   B) bbaaaa   C) bbbbaa
D) aaaaaa   E) bbbbb

10.

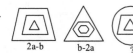

2a-b   b-2a   ?

A) b - 2a + c   B) c + a + b   C) 2c + a - b
D) c - b - a   E) c + b + a

11. $\rightarrow \frac{6}{4}$, $\rightarrow \frac{8}{6}$, $\rightarrow$?

    A) $\frac{8}{3}$ B) 2   C) $\frac{8}{6}$ D) 5   E) $\frac{8}{5}$

12. $\rightarrow$ 1, $\rightarrow$ 0, $\rightarrow$?

    A) 1   B) 2   C) 3   D) 4   E) 5

13. $\rightarrow$ 2×1, $\rightarrow$ 6×1, $\rightarrow$?

    A) 2 x 1   B) 4 x 1   C) 3 x 1   D) 3 x 3   E) 3 x 4

14. 2, 5, 11, 17, 23, ?

    A) 24   B) 25   C) 26   D) 27   E) 29

15. Find the different figure.

    A)   B)   C)

    D)   E)

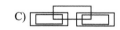

16. Find the different figure.

    A)   B)   C)

    D)   E)

17. Find the different figure.

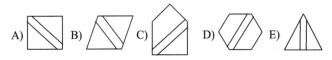

18. Find the different figure.

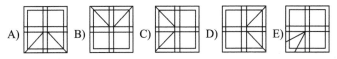

19. Find the different figure.

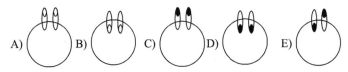

20.

▲	△	▲
⊔	▲	*
△	*	△

= ?

A) 132   B) 121   C) 121   D) 123   E) 212
    212   212   413   214   134
    331   343   232   123   321

TEST 4

1.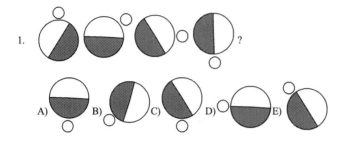

2. Find the different figure.

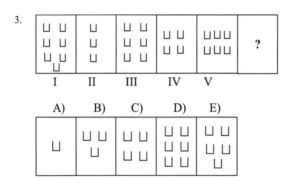

3.

4.

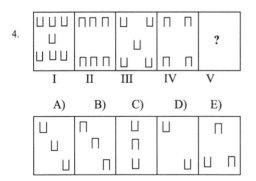

5. Find the different figure.

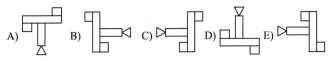

6.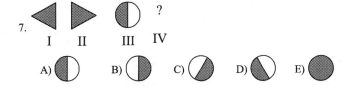

   A) 124   B) 48   C) 36   D) 32   E) 24

7.

8.

9.

10. Find the different figure.

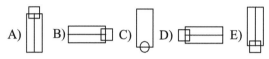

11. Find the different figure.

12.

**				****		?
	○○○	***	○ ○○○		○○ ○○○	
I	II	III	IV	V	VI	VII

A)	B)	C)	D)	E)
		○		
****	**** *		○○○○	○○○○

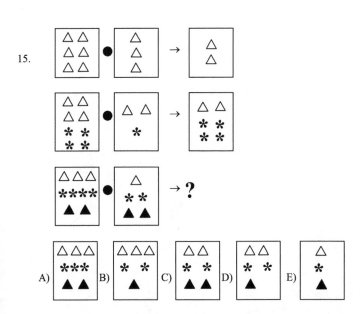

13.

I   II   III   IV

A)
B)
C)
D)
E)

14.

A) *** B) ** C) ** D) ** E) ***

15.

A) B) C) D) E)

16. 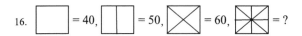 □ = 40, ▯▯ = 50, ⊠ = 60, ✳ = ?

    A) 60   B) 70   C) 80   D) 90   E) 100

17.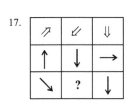

    A) ↑   B) ↖   C) ←   D) ↙   E) ↙

18.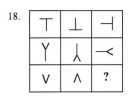

    A) V   B) ∧   C) <   D) >   E) ⊣

19. Find the different figure.

    A)   B)   C)   D)   E)

20.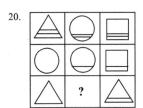

    A)   B)   C)   D)   E)

TEST 5

1.

a	b	a
m	n	m
k	l	?

A) l B) k C) a D) n E) b

2.

⊓	⊓	V
Ǝ	Λ	⊔
>	⊏	E
⊐	?	⊔

A) ⊓ B) ⊏ C) ⊓ D) < E) Λ

3.

What number should come where question mark?

A) ⌂ B) ⌂ C) ⌂ D) ⌂ E) ⌂

4.

$$\left.\begin{array}{l}\square+\triangle=7\\ \oslash+\triangle=8\\ \square+\oslash=9\end{array}\right\} \text{ and } \triangle+\square+\oslash=?$$

A) 10 B) 11 C) 12 D) 13 E) 14

5.

$$\begin{array}{r} aa\\ +bb\\ \hline 132\end{array}\quad a-b=2 \text{ and } a\cdot b=?$$

A) 36 B) 32 C) 30 D) 35 E) 34

6. △⊖□ △⊖ ○□ △⊖☑□ △○ ? □ △ ▲ ☑ △ ⊖
   What number should come where question mark?
   A) △   B) ○   C) □   D) ⊖   E) ▲

7. $a^2 \blacksquare b^2 \rightarrow a + b$
   $9\blacksquare4 \rightarrow 5$
   $16\blacksquare25 \rightarrow ?$
   A) 8   B) 9   C) 10   D) 12   E) 13

8. □ ◨ △ ⊠ ⬠ ?
   A) ⊕   B) ⊕   C) ⬡   D) ⬡   E) ◿

9.

Circle segments: ? , 10, 136, 12, 72, 16, 40, 24

   A) 186   B) 208   C) 225   D) 264   E) 288

10.

A	A	L
A	L	A
L	A	?

   A) A   B) A   C) A   D) A   E) A

11.

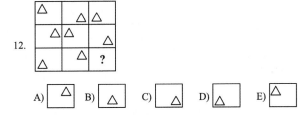

12.

13.

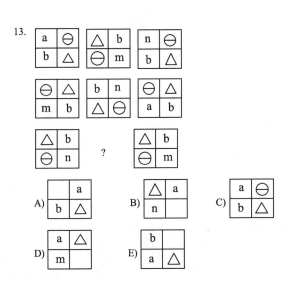

14.

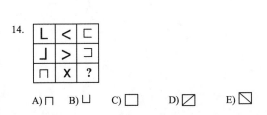

A)⊓   B)⊔   C)☐   D)◩   E)◲

15.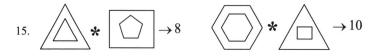

 → ?

A) 6   B) 7   C) 8   D) 9   E)10

16.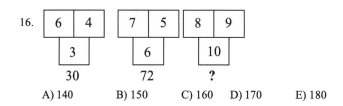

A) 140   B) 150   C) 160   D) 170   E) 180

17.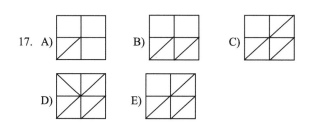

18. Find the different figure.

A)

B)

C)

D)

E)

19. Find the different figure.

A)

B)

C)

D)

E)

20.

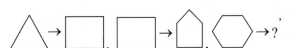

A)

B)

C)

D)

E)

TEST 6

1.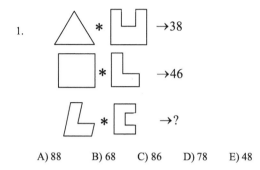

   A) 88   B) 68   C) 86   D) 78   E) 48

2.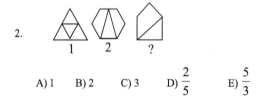

   A) 1   B) 2   C) 3   D) $\dfrac{2}{5}$ E) $\dfrac{5}{3}$

3.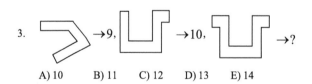

   A) 10   B) 11   C) 12   D) 13   E) 14

4.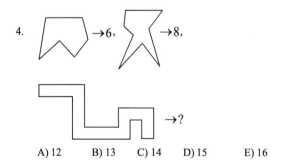

   A) 12   B) 13   C) 14   D) 15   E) 16

5.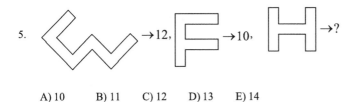

A) 10   B) 11   C) 12   D) 13   E) 14

6.
```
▲   ▲△   △▲△   △▲△▲
▲   ▲△   △▲△   △▲▲▲   ?
▲   ▲△   △▲△   △▲▲▲
I    II     III       IV        V
```

A)
```
▲▲▲
△△△
▲▲▲
△△△
△△△
```
B)
```
▲△▲▲ ▲
▲△▲▲ ▲
▲△▲△ ▲
```
C)
```
△▲△
△▲△
△▲△
```

D)
```
△△▲▲
△△▲▲
△△▲▲
```
E)
```
▲▲▲▲
△△△△
▲▲▲▲
```

7. L * V →36, ⌐ * L →48,

N * F →?

A) 90   B) 95   C) 80   D) 70   E) 60

8.
```
        39  27
         *→*
   *→*       *→*
   68  48    48   ?
```
A) 24   B) 32   C) 23   D) 24   E) 30

9.

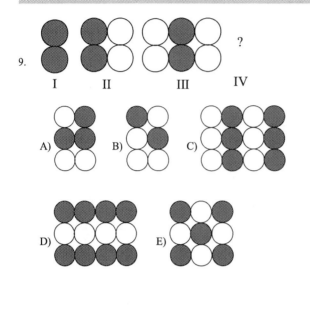

10.

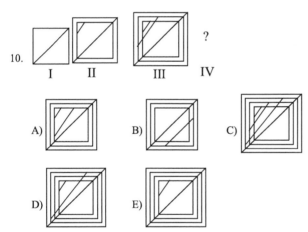

11.

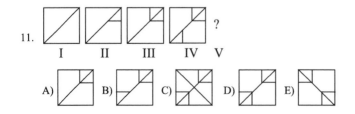

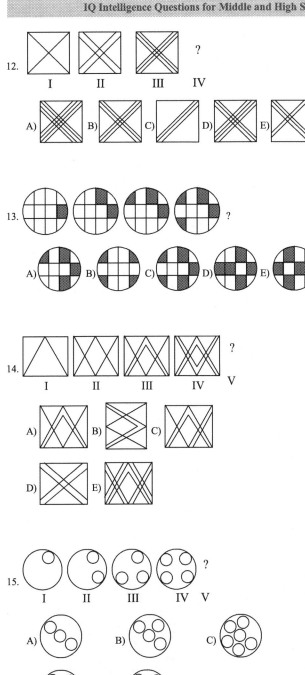

16.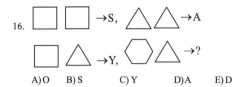

A) O   B) S   C) Y   D) A   E) D

17.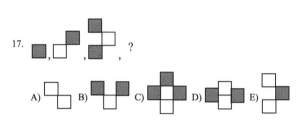

A)   B)   C)   D)   E)

18. Find the different figure.

19.

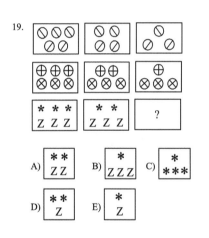

A)   B)   C)

D)   E)

20.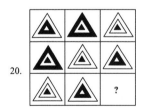

A)   B)   C)   D)   E)

TEST 7

1.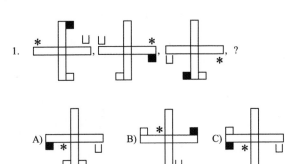

A)   B)   C)

D)   E)

2.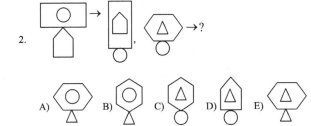

A)   B)   C)   D)   E)

3.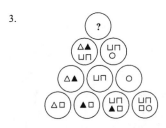

A) ⊔⊓O△   B) △▲O   C) △▲⊔

D) ⊔⊓●   E) ⊔⊓O

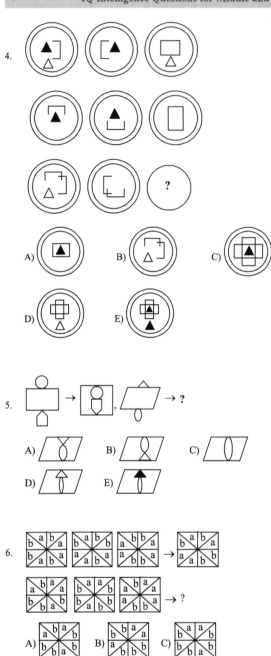

7.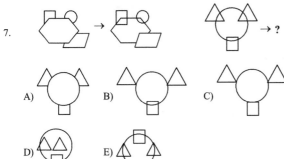

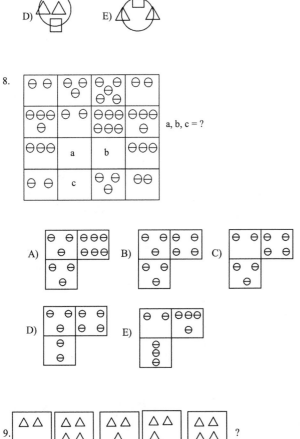

8.

a, b, c = ?

9.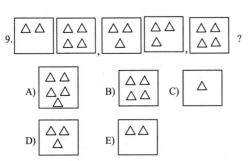

10. Find the different figure.

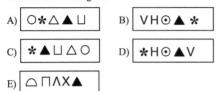

A) ○✻△▲⊔   B) VH⊙▲✻

C) ✻▲⊔△○   D) ✻H⊙▲V

E) △⊓∧X▲

11.

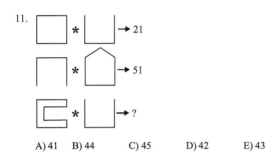

A) 41   B) 44   C) 45   D) 42   E) 43

12.

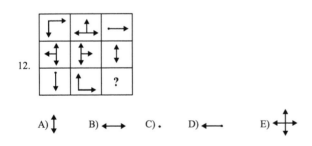

A) ↕   B) ↔   C) •   D) ←   E) ↔↕

13.

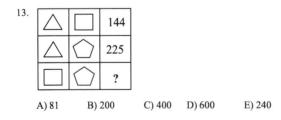

A) 81   B) 200   C) 400   D) 600   E) 240

14.

A) ↖   B) →   C) ←   D) ↘   E) ↗

15.

3	2	4	5
4	3	5	6
24	12	40	60
6	3	10	x

A) 10   B) 12   C) 13   D) 14   E) 15

16.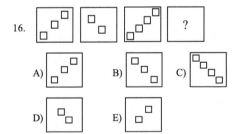

17. ▲ ▲ △ → 2 − 1
     ▲ ▲ ▲ → 3 + 0
     ■ ■ ■ □ → ?

A) 3 + 1   B) 3 + 10   C) 4 + 1   D) 3 − 1   E) 3 − 10

18.

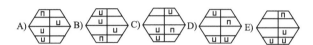

A) 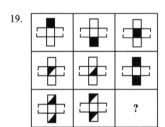 B) C) D) E)

19.

A) B) C) D) E)

20.

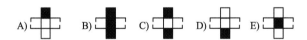

What number should come where question mark?

A) ⊔   B) ⊘   C) ⊘   D) ⊖   E) ⊓

TEST 8

1. ⌂ − □ = 12
   □ + ▲ = 16   and ■ = ?
   ⌂ + ▲ = ■ + ■

   A) 6   B) 8   C) 14   D) 10   E) 11

2.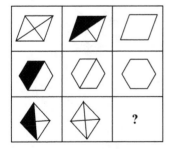

   A)   B)   C)   D) 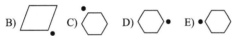   E)

3.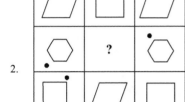

4. △ △ : △ = □ □ and □ + □ = ?
   A) 2   B) 3   C) 4   D) 6   E) 8

5.

A) ↓   B) ←   C) →   D) ↑   E) ↙

6.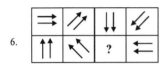

A) ↓↓   B) ⇐   C) ⇒   D) ↑↑   E) ↘↘

7. 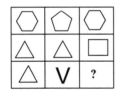 → ?

A) 113	B) 131	C) 132	D) 233	E) 123
312	213	213	121	312
312	322	123	321	231

8.

⬡	⬠	⬡
△	△	□
△	V	?

A) V   B) △   C) □   D) ▱   E) ◇

9.

A) 3   B) 2   C) 1   D) 4   E) 21

10.

A) □   B) △   C) ⌂   D) ⬡   E) ⊠

11.

A) △   B) □   C) ⌂   D) ⬡   E) ▱

12.

52	84	43	72
△	□	⬡	?

A) △   B) □   C) ⬡   D) ⌂   E) Λ

13.

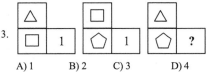

A) 1   B) 2   C) 3   D) 4   E) 5

14.

△△	△△	○○
ΛΛ	ΛΛ	□□
VV	△△	?

A) □□   B) △△   C) ⬠⬠   D) ΛΛ   E) ○○

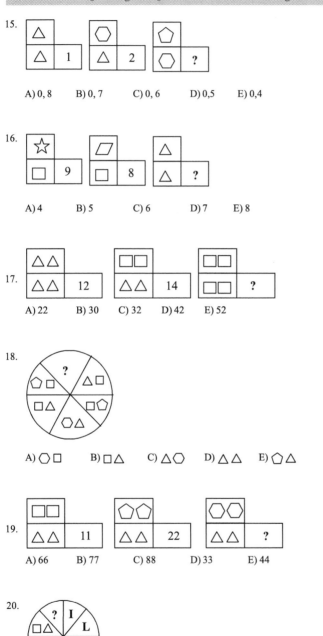

15.

A) 0, 8   B) 0, 7   C) 0, 6   D) 0,5   E) 0,4

16.

A) 4   B) 5   C) 6   D) 7   E) 8

17.

A) 22   B) 30   C) 32   D) 42   E) 52

18.

A) ⬡ ☐   B) ☐ △   C) △ ◯   D) △ △   E) ⬠ △

19.

A) 66   B) 77   C) 88   D) 33   E) 44

20.

A) ☐ △   B) △ △   C) ☐ ☐   D) ⬡ △   E) △

TEST 9

1. 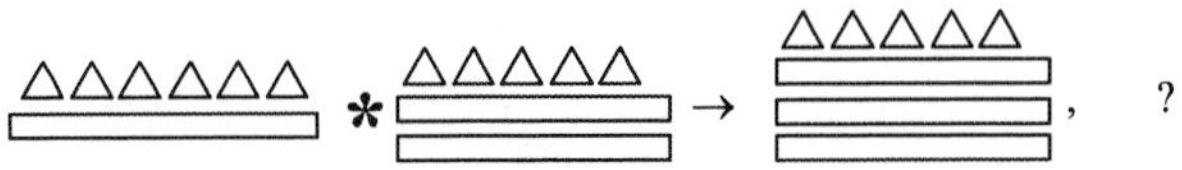 △△△△△△ ⬚ * △△△△△ ⬚ → △△△△△ ⬚ , ?

A)  △△△ ⬚ B) 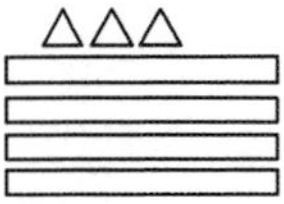 △△△ ⬚ C) 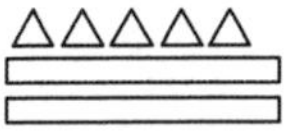 △△△△△ ⬚

D) 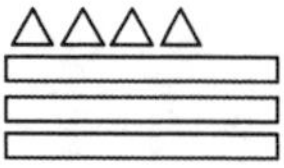 △△△△ ⬚

E) 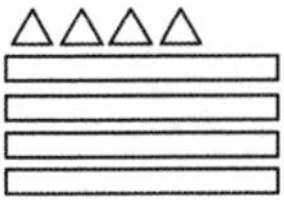 △△△△ ⬚

2.

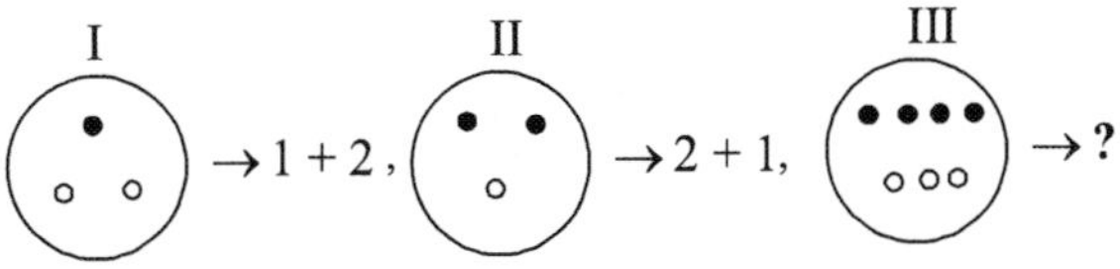

I $\bigcirc$ → 1 + 2 , II $\bigcirc$ → 2 + 1 , III $\bigcirc$ → ?

A) 3 + 4   B) 4 + 3   C) 3 + 3   D) 4 + 2   E) 2 + 4

3. 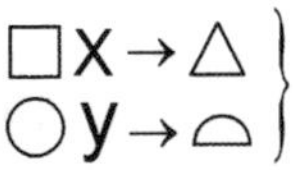 $\square x \to \triangle$
   $\bigcirc y \to \frown$ and $x + y = ?$

A) 1   B) $\dfrac{1}{2}$ C) $\dfrac{1}{3}$ D) $\dfrac{2}{3}$ E) $\dfrac{3}{2}$

4.

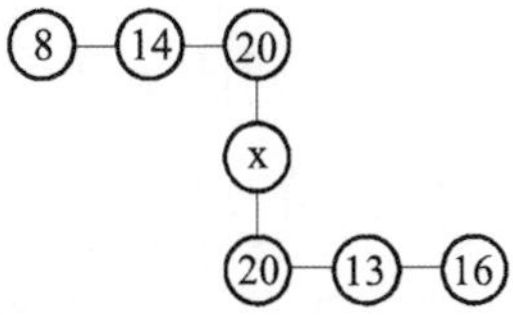

⑧—⑭—⑳
        Ⓧ
⑳—⑬—⑯

A) 20   B) 22   C) 24   D) 26   E) 28

5. 20.

14	36
27	94

49	72
63	41

ab	cd
kl	mn

?

A)
nm	lk
cd	ba

B)
nm	lk
kl	ba

C)
nm	lk
dc	ba

D)
ba	dc
lk	nm

E)
ba	kl
cd	nm

6.

    I   II   III   IV

?

A)   B)   C)   D)   E)

7.
$$\square + \triangle = 6$$
$$\triangle - 3 = \bigcirc$$
$$\square \times \bigcirc = \square$$
and $\square + \triangle + \bigcirc = ?$

A) 6   B) 7   C) 8   D) 10   E) 12

8.
$$\square + 2 = \triangle$$
$$\bigcirc \div \square = 2$$
$$\bigcirc + \triangle = 11$$
and $\bigcirc = ?$

A) 3   B) 5   C) 6   D) 8   E) 10

9.
$$\square + \triangle = 20$$
$$\bigcirc - \triangle = 10$$
and $\square + \bigcirc = ?$

A) 20   B) 30   C) 50   D) 25   E) 36

10. Find the different figure.

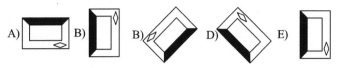

11. $2\triangle + 2\triangle + 2\triangle = \blacksquare$ $2\blacktriangle + 2\blacktriangle + 2\blacktriangle = \blacktriangle + \blacktriangle$

$\blacktriangle : \triangle = ?$

A) 5   B) 4   C) 3   D) 2   E) 1

12. 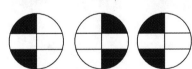 $= ?$

A) 565	B) 575	C) 465	D) 565	E) 654
657	767	675	765	456
765	765	764	756	374

13.

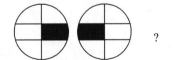

?

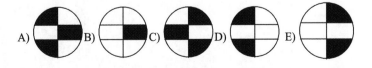

A)   B)   C)   D)   E)

14. ⬡ ⬠ ☐ △ → 7654

△ ⬠ ☐ ⬡ → ?

A) 3556   B) 3557   C) 4657   D) 7564   E) 3643

15. A: 4, 7, 10, 13, 16
    B: 5, 9, 13, 17, 21
    C: 20, 17, 14, 11, 8
    D: ?
    A) 24, 23, 20, 17   B) 28, 24, 20, 16   C) 28, 24, 20, 16, 12
    D) 30, 36, 32, 28, 20   E) 20, 16, 12, 8, 6

16. A: 4, 9, 16, 25
    B: 1, 8, 27, 64
    C: 36, 49, 64, 81
    D: ?
    A) 25, 36, 9, 64   B) 125, 36, 343, 152   C) 125, 216, 343, 512
    D) 124, 215, 343, 511   E) 123, 216, 343, 510

17. A: 2, 3, 4, 5
    B: 4, 9, 16, 25
    C: 5, 6, 7, 8
    D: ?
    A) 64, 49, 36, 24   B) 25, 36, 49, 64   C) 25, 18, 49, 10
    D) 25, 36, 48, 64   E) 24, 48, 36, 81

18. A: 2, 5, 7, 8
    B: 9, 36, 64, 81
    C: 4, 5, 6, 7
    D: ?
    A) 25, 36, 36, 49   B) 49, 36, 24, 16   C) 25, 36, 49, 64
    D) 25, 35, 45, 65   E) 24, 34, 44, 64

19. A: 3, 5, 7, 9
    B: 15, 35, 63
    C: 8, 9, 10, 5
    D: ?
    A) 72, 90, 50   B) 70, 90, 50   C) 71, 89, 49
    D) 73, 88, 48   E) 30, 40, 50, 60

20. A: 5, 6, 7, 2
    B: 30, 42, 14
    C: 2, 4, 8, 5
    D. ?
    A) 8, 32, 42   B) 8, 31, 40   C) 6, 32, 40
    D) 8, 30, 42   E) 8, 32, 40

TEST 10

1. A: 30, 42, 84, 16
    B: 15, 21, 42, 8
    C: 40, 30, 12, 4
    D: ?
    A) 40, 15, 6, 2   B) 40, 30, 6, 2   C) 30, 20, 6, 4
    D) 20, 15, 6, 2   E) 20, 16, 7, 4

2. A: 64, 80, 40, 16
    B: 16, 20, 10, 4
    C: 40, 36, 12, 4
    D: ?
    A) 5, 4, 4, 4   B) 4, 4, 3, 4   C) 10, 9, 3, 1
    D) 5, 4, 4, 4   E) 6, 7, 2, 4

3. A: 3, 4, 5, 6
    B: 12, 20, 30
    C: 6, 4, 5, 7
    D: ?
    A) 24, 20, 30   B) 20, 24, 30   C) 22, 21, 35
    D) 24, 20, 35   E) 24, 16, 36

4. 12, 4, 16, 24, 8, 64, 21, 7, x
    A) 46   B) 47   C) 48   D) 49   E) 51

5. A: 2, 3, 5, 7, 11
    B: 4, 6, 10, 14, 22
    C: 13, 17, 19, 23
    D: ?
    A) 10, 12, 14, 16   B) 12, 16, 18, 20   C) 12, 16, 19, 20
    D) 26, 34, 38, 46   E) 12, 16, 18, 20

6. A: 6, 8, 10, 12, 14
    B: 7, 9, 11, 13, 15
    C: 10, 12, 14, 20, 22
    D: ?
    A) 11, 12, 17, 11, 16   B) 11, 13, 12, 13, 15 C) 11, 13, 15, 17, 19
    D) 11, 14, 13, 22, 25   E) 14, 15, 16, 17

7. A: 5, 10, 15, 20
    B: 30, 35, 40, 45
    C: 50, 55, 60, 65
    D: ?
    A) 70, 75, 65, 45   B) 70, 75, 80, 85   C) 45, 50, 54, 59
    D) 70, 75, 74, 80   E) 40, 44, 45, 46

8. 5, 10, 20, 25, 50, ?
    A) 52   B) 55   C) 60   D) 62   E) 72

9. 3, 8, 15, 24, ?
    A) 30,   B) 32   C) 33   D) 34   E) 35

10. 24, 35, 48, 63, ?
    A) 80   B) 81   C) 82   D) 83   E) 84

11. 11, 13, 17, 19, ?
    A) 20,   B) 21,   C) 22   D) 23   E) 25

12. 6, 7, 10, 11 ,12, 13, 15, ?
    A) 16   B) 17   C) 18   D) 19   E) 20

13. 2, 3, 6, 18, 108, ?
    A) 1844   B) 1744   C) 1644   D) 1544   E) 1944

14. 4, 5, 20, 21, 105, ?
    A) 106   B) 107   C) 515   D) 525   E) 425

15. $\triangle^{\triangle} \to 27$, $\square^{\square} \to$?

    A) 16   B) 32   C) 64   D) 68   E) 51

16. $(\triangle)^{\square} \to 81$, $(\square)^{\triangle} \to$?
    A) 16   B) 32   C) 36   D) 64   E) 128

17. $\left. \begin{array}{l} \square \bigstar \to 39 \\ \triangle \bigstar \to 26 \end{array} \right\}$ $\square + \bigstar + \triangle =$?
    A) 16   B) 17   C) 18   D) 19   E) 20

18.

$\boxed{10}$ $\boxed{15}$ $x = ?$
12×5 $25 \times x$
$\boxed{6}$ $\boxed{5}$

A) 2   B) 3   C) 4   D) 5   E) 6

19.

▲ ● ○ ⎫
○ □ ○ ⎪ ⎧ 123
○ ■ ✲ ⎬ ⇒ ⎨ 343
▲ ● ✲ ⎭ ⎩ 345
             125

$(x + \blacksquare + \bigcirc) - (\blacktriangle + \bullet) = ?$

A) 9   B) 8   C) 10   D) 11   E) 7

20. ▲ + ● = 22

■ + ▲ = 24

● + ■ = 26

■ + ▲ + ● = ?

A) 36   B) 47   C) 50   D) 70   E) 72

TEST 11

1. 7, 10, 20, 23, 46, ?
   A) 48   B) 49   C) 50   D) 51   E) 52

2.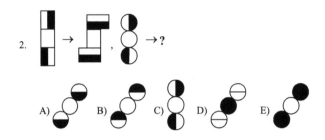

3.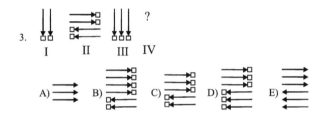

4.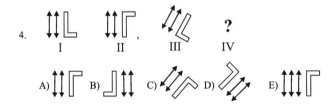

5. Find the different figure.

   A)  B) C) D) E)

6. Find the different figure.

   A) B) C) D) E)

7. Find the different figure.

A)   B)   C)   D) 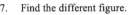 E)

8. Find the different figure.

A) ■ B) ◀◀ C) ▶▶ D) ▶▶▌ E) ▌◀◀

9. Which picture should be in place of the question mark?

A)   B)   C) ⊞ D) ✕ E) ◣

10. Which picture should be in place of the question mark?

A)   B)   C) 🖐 D) ☝ E) 𝄞

11. Find the different figure.

A) ☆ B) ❀ C) ✳ D) ☆ E) ★

12. Find the different figure.

A) ⊙ B) ▣ C) ▣ D) ▪ E) ■

13. Find the different figure.

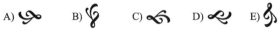

A)   B)   C)   D)   E)

14. Find the different figure.

A)   B)   C)   D)   E)

15. 14, 20, 19, 17, 12, ?
    20, 26, 25, 23, 18, ?
    A) 11   B) 11   C) 12   D) 9   E) 7
       17   16   17   14   12

16. 24,   36,   44,   66,   27
     6,   9,   8,   12,   ?
    A) 6   B) 7   C) 8   D) 9   E) 11

17. 124, 336, 121, 144, 125
     8,   54,   2,   16, ?
    A) 10   B) 11   C) 12   D) 13   E) 20

18. 123, 644, 120, 244, 484
     4 , 16,   0,   6,   ?
    A) 0   B) 2   C) 10   D) 11   E) 12

19. 8, 24, 9, 27, 40, ?
    A) 120   B) 121   C) 80   D) 90   E) 110

20. 120, 60, 20, 5, ?
    A) 6   B) 5   C) 4   D) 3   E) 1

TEST 12

1. $\dfrac{2}{3}, \dfrac{4}{4}, \dfrac{16}{5}, ?$

   A) $\dfrac{32}{5}$ B) $\dfrac{64}{6}$ C) $\dfrac{68}{6}$ D) $\dfrac{256}{6}$ E) $\dfrac{156}{6}$

2. $\dfrac{3}{2}, \dfrac{4}{4}, \dfrac{5}{8}, \dfrac{6}{16}, ?$

   A) $\dfrac{7}{16}$ B) $\dfrac{7}{15}$ C) $\dfrac{7}{32}$ D) $\dfrac{7}{64}$ E) $\dfrac{7}{62}$

3. $\dfrac{1}{2}, \dfrac{1}{4}, \dfrac{2}{3}, \dfrac{4}{9}, \dfrac{6}{5}, ?$

   A) $\dfrac{30}{25}$ B) $\dfrac{30}{24}$ C) $\dfrac{25}{36}$ D) $\dfrac{36}{25}$ E) $\dfrac{36}{22}$

4. $\dfrac{4}{7}, \dfrac{11}{8}, \dfrac{19}{9}, \dfrac{28}{10}, ?$

   A) $\dfrac{37}{11}$ B) $\dfrac{38}{11}$ C) $\dfrac{38}{10}$ D) $\dfrac{38}{10}$ E) $\dfrac{27}{12}$

5. 642, 264, 843, 384, 721, ?

   A) 171   B) 172   C) 173   D) 271   E) 272

6. 437, 347, 621, 261, 124, ?
   A) 213   B) 214   C) 412   D) 241   E) 145

7. abc, bca, def, edf, kmn, ?
   A) kmn   B) mnk   C) mkn   D) knm   E) nmkn

8. $\dfrac{1}{\sqrt{3}}, \dfrac{1}{3}, \dfrac{1}{\sqrt{5}}, \dfrac{1}{5}, \dfrac{2}{\sqrt{7}},$?

    A) $\dfrac{2}{7}$ B) $\dfrac{12}{7}$ C) $\dfrac{4}{7}$ D) $\dfrac{2}{9}$ E) $\dfrac{7}{2}$

9. $\dfrac{2}{\sqrt{3}}, \dfrac{\sqrt{2}}{3}, \dfrac{3}{\sqrt{5}}, \dfrac{\sqrt{3}}{5}, \dfrac{6}{\sqrt{3}},$?

    A) $\dfrac{\sqrt{6}}{\sqrt{3}}$ B) $\dfrac{\sqrt{6}}{2}$ C) $\dfrac{\sqrt{6}}{3}$ D) $\dfrac{\sqrt{7}}{2}$ E) $\dfrac{36}{\sqrt{3}}$

10. $\dfrac{1}{3}, \dfrac{3}{4}, \dfrac{12}{5}, \dfrac{60}{6},$?

    A) $\dfrac{370}{6}$ B) $\dfrac{360}{7}$ C) $\dfrac{360}{6}$ D) $\dfrac{380}{6}$ E) $\dfrac{366}{6}$

11. Find the different figure.
     A) 12   B) 24   C) 48   D) 35   E) 66

12. I   6,   4,   24
     II   8,   1,   8
     III ?   ?   ?
     A) 6, 4, 20   B) 6, 4, 22   C) 7, 3, 21   D) 8, 4, 36   E) 7, 4, 27

13. A: 7, 21, 20, 60, 59
     B: ?
     A) 6, 18, 17, 54, 52, 104   B) 6, 18, 52, 50, 100   C) 8, 24, 23, 69, 68
     D) 3, 9, 8, 24, 22, 66   E) 5, 15, 14, 42, 84

14. 44   (16)   12
     28   (4)   20
     144   (x)   44
     A) 30   B) 40   C) 50   D) 60   E) 70

15.

    A)   B)   C)   D)   E)

16.

    A) 🍵   B) ◣   C) ⊖   D) ?   E) ⊠

17.

    A) 🐚   B) ✿   C) 〰   D) ?   E) ⊖

18.

    A) ☺   B) ●   C) ☹   D) ♪   E) ♬

19.

    A) ✏   B) ✎   C) ✗   D) ✔   E) ♪

20. $6412 \rightarrow 10;3$
    $1473 \rightarrow 5;10$
    $3764 \rightarrow ?; ?$
    A) 10; 4   B) 10; 6   C) 6; 10   D) 10; 8   E) 10; 10

TEST 13

9. Find the different picture.

10. 3, 7, 14, 18, 36, 40, 80, ?
    What number should come where question mark?

    A) 82   B) 84   C) 164   D) 160   E) 164

3. $423 \rightarrow 6; 5$
   $715 \rightarrow 8;6$
   $316 \rightarrow ?; ?$
   A) 4; 6   B) 6; 4   C) 3; 7   D) 4; 7   E) 7; 4

4. $423 \rightarrow 8; 6$
   $825 \rightarrow 16; 10$
   $326 \rightarrow ?$
   A) 6; 8   B) 6; 10   C) 6; 12   D) 16; 6   E) 8; 6

5. $124 \rightarrow 8$
   $123 \rightarrow 6$
   $723 \rightarrow ?$
   A) 14   B) 28   C) 32   D) 42   E) 84

6. $729 \rightarrow 0$
   $824 \rightarrow 6$
   $713 \rightarrow 5$
   $515 \rightarrow ?$
   A) 1   B) 2   C) 3   D) 4   E) 5

7. $1624 \rightarrow 3$
   $2435 \rightarrow 6$
   $9876 \rightarrow 0$
   $9816 \rightarrow ?$
   A) 2   B) 3   C) 6   D) 5   E) 4

8. $2412 \rightarrow 2$
   $3618 \rightarrow 2$
   $9045 \rightarrow 2$
   $2804 \rightarrow ?$
   A) 6   B) 7   C) 8   D) 9   E) 10

9. $(3\triangle 4)\square 24 \rightarrow 1$
   $(1\triangle 3)\square 9 \rightarrow 1$
   $(3\triangle 2)\square 2 \rightarrow ?$
   A) 11   B) 8   C) 7   D) 6   E) 9

10. $(3\triangle 4)\blacksquare 25 \rightarrow 50$
    $(1\triangle 4)\blacksquare 16 \rightarrow 33$
    $(2\triangle 3)\blacksquare 12 \rightarrow ?$
    A) 20   B) 21   C) 23   D) 24   E) 25

11. $(2\triangle 3)*2 \rightarrow 36$
    $(1\triangle 4)*2 \rightarrow 16$
    $(2\triangle 7)*2 \rightarrow ?$
    A) 142   B) 143   C) 196   D) 146   E) 200

12. $(6\blacktriangle 8)*(6\blacktriangle 3) \rightarrow 30$
    $(3\blacktriangle 12)*(3\blacktriangle 4) \rightarrow 24$
    $(7\blacktriangle 3)*(4\blacktriangle 2) \rightarrow ?$
    A) 10   B) 11   C) 12   D) 13   E) 14

13. $(6*8)\triangle(8\triangle 4) \rightarrow 24$
    $(6*4)\triangle(9\triangle 3) \rightarrow 8$
    $(12*3)\triangle(24\triangle 3) \rightarrow ?$

    A) 4   B) 6   C) 7   D) 8   E) $\dfrac{9}{2}$

14. $(6\square 4)*(8\blacksquare 4) \rightarrow 4$
    $(9\square 3)*(7\blacksquare 2) \rightarrow 21$
    $(10\square 6)*(14\blacksquare 4) \rightarrow ?$
    A) 11   B) 12   C) 13   D) 14   E) 15

15. abcd
    ecdf
    becq   bcda = ?
    cdeq
    bcda
    A) 1234   B) 2341   C) 2536   D) 3456   E) 5347

16. 12323
    42525
    63535⎬   and   63535 = ?
    53536
    32533

    A) □∗△∗△   B) ○∗⊕∗⊕   C) ▲△⊕△⊕
    D) ⊕△⊕△▲   E) △∗⊕△△

17. 12324 ⎫ △▲□∗○
    52124 ⎬ □∗△∗▲   62341 = ?
    34126 ⎭ ■∗□∗▲
    A) ○△□∗○   B) ○∗△▲□   C) □▲△∗○   D) ■∗□∗▲   E) ○∗△▲●

18. 1234⎫ ∗△□■
    4321⎪ ∗⊕□∗
    5612⎬ □⊕△∗   and   ⊕○□ △∗ = ?
    3621⎪ ○⊕∗△
    1631⎭ ■□△∗
    A) 65421   B) 56421   C) 45212   D) 45421   E) 65321

19. 7236
    8314
    9583⎬   and   9583 = ?
    1214
    4326

    A) 3870   B) 2745   C) 1427   D) 9895   E) 5780

20. abced⎫ 25431
    cbaed⎪ 51324
    edcba⎬ 54321   cbaed = ?
    eacbd⎪ 32154
    bedca⎭ 12354

    A) 12354   B) 32154   C) 54321   D) 51324   E) 25431

TEST 14

1.
$$\left.\begin{array}{l} \text{prmn} \\ \text{mnpr} \\ \text{mrpn} \\ \text{nprm} \\ \text{pnmr} \end{array}\right\} \text{and} \quad \text{pnmr} = ?$$

A) 2864   B) 8246   C) 6428 D) 6824   E) 2468

2.
$$\left.\begin{array}{l} 1234 \\ 3412 \\ 5123 \\ 3412 \\ 1354 \end{array}\right\} \quad 5123 = ?$$

A) $+* < \#$ B) $< \#+*$ C) $\$+* <$ D) $< \#+*$ E) $+ < \$\#$

3.
$$\left.\begin{array}{l} 6798 \\ 7986 \\ 9867 \\ 7698 \\ 9668 \end{array}\right\} \text{and} \quad 9867 = ?$$

A) $\in **\#$ B) $< * \in \#$ C) $\in \#* <$ D) $< \in \#*$ E) $* < \in \#$

4.
$$\left.\begin{array}{l} 123 \\ 456 \\ 634 \\ 434 \\ 251 \end{array}\right\} \text{and} \quad 634 = ?$$

A) $\#* \in$ B) $<> \$$ C) $\$\in <$ D) $< \in <$ E) $* > \#$

5.
$$\left.\begin{array}{l} \text{abc} \\ \text{cba} \\ \text{bbc} \\ \text{bad} \\ \text{dac} \end{array}\right\} \text{and} \quad \text{bad} = ?$$

A) $*\triangle\#$ B) $< *\#$ C) $\triangle* <$ D) $\triangle\triangle\#$ E) $\#\triangle*$

6.
$$\left.\begin{array}{l} aba \\ ata \\ ava \\ tat \end{array}\right\}$$ and tab = ?

A) □△□   B) □✳□   C) □▲□   D) ■□■   E) ■□△

7.
$$\left.\begin{array}{l} 123 \\ 321 \\ 654 \\ 125 \\ 534 \end{array}\right\}$$ and 321 = ?

A) 643   B) 216   C) 763   D) 412   E) 217

8.
$$\left.\begin{array}{l} 124 \\ 421 \\ 356 \\ 653 \\ 514 \end{array}\right\}$$ and 356 = ?

A) 623   B) 564   C) 465   D) 312   E) 213

9.
$$\left.\begin{array}{l} 136 \\ 789 \\ 125 \\ 624 \\ 534 \end{array}\right\}$$ and 125 = ?

A) 970   B) 321   C) 984   D) 085   E) 475

10.
$$\left.\begin{array}{l} 950 \\ 840 \\ 321 \\ 489 \\ 673 \end{array}\right\}$$ and 321 = ?

A) 762   B) 845   C) 230   D) 481   E) 591

11. $\left.\begin{array}{l} 124 \\ 672 \\ 942 \\ 125 \\ 336 \end{array}\right\}$ and 125 = ?

    A) 038   B) 763   C) 583   D) 039   E) 227

12. $\left.\begin{array}{l} 984 \\ 436 \\ 541 \\ 123 \\ 455 \end{array}\right\}$ and 123 = ?

    A) 544   B) 032   C) 450   D) 527   E) 895

13. $\left.\begin{array}{l} 123 \\ 465 \\ 789 \\ 912 \\ 6\ 21 \end{array}\right\}$ and 465 = ?

    A) 069   B) 524   C) 873   D) 306   E) 260

14. $\left.\begin{array}{l} 912 \\ 765 \\ 423 \\ 840 \\ 762 \end{array}\right\}$ and 840 = ?

    A) 021   B) 856   C) 314   D) 739   E) 851

15. 321
    456
    789
    781 = ?
    426
    A) #b△   B) * < a   C) * <>   D) #$△   E) cba

16. 912   = ?
    876
    543
    321
    821

    A) > ab   B) < *△   C) $ # <   D) cba   E) < ba

17. 128
    764   = ?
    523
    321
    478

    A) abc   B) def   C) hbs   D) sba   E) fdc

18.
    mab ⎫
    myz ⎪
    dbc ⎬ and   yzm = ?
    yzm ⎪
    xcd ⎭

    A) 812   B) 867   C) 423   D) 678   E) 534

19. 082
    324
    567   = ?
    980
    790

    A) 128   B) 987   C) 654   D) 321   E) 431

20. 822
    794
    356   = ?
    343
    189

    A) 023   B) 939   C) 965   D) 437   E) 288

TEST 15

1. 123
   422
   579   = ?
   835
   448
   A) 339   B) 942   C) 218   D) 355   E) 754

2. 165
   234
   651   = ?
   433
   255
   A) △■□   B) ○⊕▲   C) ■□△   D) ▲⊕⊕   E) ○□□

3. 414
   313
   587   =?
   654
   215
   A) ▲△▲   B) ⊕△⊕   C) □*●   D) ■□▲   E) ○△□

4. 321
   431
   865
   786
   123   = ?
   A) ⊕○△   B) ▲⊕△   C) *■□   D) ●*■   E) △○⊕

5.
   (x)
   (96) (432)
   (4) (24) (18)
   (1) (4) (6) (3)

   A) 41372   B) 41362   C) 41472
   D) 42472   E) 43472

6. $a \square b \rightarrow a^b - b^a$ and $(3\square1)\square(1\square2)$

   A) 1   B) $-\dfrac{1}{2}$ C) $\dfrac{1}{2}$ D) $\dfrac{3}{2}$ E) $\dfrac{5}{2}$

7.
$$\begin{array}{|cc|} 2 & 3 \\ 7 & 5 \end{array} \quad \begin{array}{|cc|} 11 & 13 \\ 19 & 17 \end{array} \quad \begin{array}{|cc|} 23 & 29 \\ x & 31 \end{array} \quad x = ?$$

A) 32   B) 33   C) 34   D) 36   E) 37

8.
$$\begin{array}{|cc|} 6 & 12 \\ 2 & 4 \end{array} \quad \begin{array}{|cc|} 6 & 12 \\ x & 8 \end{array} \quad x = ?$$

A) 2   B) 3   C) 4   D) 6   E) 7

9.
$$\begin{array}{|cc|} \frac{1}{2} & 6 \\ 216 & \frac{1}{8} \end{array} \quad \begin{array}{|cc|} 4 & 2 \\ 8 & 64 \end{array} \quad \begin{array}{|cc|} x & 3 \\ 27 & 5 \end{array} \quad x = ?$$

A) 25   B) 125   C) 124   D) 130   E) 625

10.
$$\begin{array}{|cc|} 4 & 5 \\ \boxed{4} & \\ 1 & 6 \end{array} \quad \begin{array}{|cc|} 7 & 10 \\ \boxed{5} & \\ 8 & 0 \end{array} \quad \begin{array}{|cc|} 10 & 11 \\ \boxed{6} & \\ 5 & x \end{array} \quad x = ?$$

A) 10   B) 15   C) 16   D) 20   E) 25

11.
$$\begin{array}{|cc|} 1 & 4 \\ ② & \\ 0 & 3 \end{array} \quad \begin{array}{|cc|} 10 & 7 \\ ③ & \\ 4 & 6 \end{array} \quad \begin{array}{|cc|} 20 & 30 \\ ④ & \\ 4 & x \end{array} \quad x = ?$$

A) 10   B) 11   C) 12   D) 16   E) 18

12.
$$\begin{array}{|cc|} 6 & 9 \\ 2 & 3 \end{array} \quad \begin{array}{|cc|} 5 & 10 \\ 2 & 4 \end{array} \quad \begin{array}{|cc|} 18 & 9 \\ x & 2 \end{array} \quad x = ?$$

A) 4   B) 5   C) 6   D) 7   E) 8

13.
$$\begin{array}{|c|} 18 \\ 3 \times 24 \\ 4 \end{array} \quad \begin{array}{|c|} 15 \\ 2 \times 30 \\ 4 \end{array} \quad \begin{array}{|c|} 20 \\ x \times 40 \\ 4 \end{array} \quad x = ?$$

A) 2   B) 3   C) 4   D) 6   E) 10

14.
9 / 12 \ 4 / 3	12 / 16 \ 4 / 3	6 / 2 \ 7 / x

$x = ?$

A) 10   B) 11   C) 20   D) 21   E) 23

15.
2 / 5 \ 7 / 3	11 / 19 \ 17 / 13	23 / x \ 31 / 29

$x = ?$

A) 34   B) 35   C) 36   D) 37   E) 39

2	4
8	6

2	5
11	8

2	x_1
x_2	x_3

16. $x_1 = ?$
A) 6   B) 8   C) 10   D) 11   E) 12

17. $x_2 = ?$
A) 10   B) 14   C) 12   D) 16   E) 18

18. $x_3 = ?$
A) 10   B) 11   C) 12   D) 13   E) 14

19.
4	6 / 16
2 / 1	3

2	2 / 1
15 / 30	2

2	2 / 5
20 / 16	x

$x = ?$

A) 5   B) 4   C) 3   D) 2   E) 1

20.
8	6	$\sqrt{12}$
11	9	x
14	12	$\sqrt{48}$

$x = ?$

A) $2\sqrt{3}$ B) $3\sqrt{3}$ C) $4\sqrt{3}$ D) $5\sqrt{3}$ E) $\sqrt{3}$

TEST 16

1.
6	12	8
8	10	7
10	2	x

x = ?

A) 8   B) 9   C) 10   D) 11   E) 12

2.
3	12	36
4	16	64
121	x	121

x = ?

A) 5   B) 4   C) 3   D) 2   E) 1

3.

x = ?

A) 20   B) 21   C) 24   D) 26   E) 28

4.
4	5		2	4		7	6
26	17		65	9		37	x

x = ?

A) 49   B) 50   C) 51   D) 52   E) 53

5.
4	5		6	7
17	14		x	20

x = ?

A) 20   B) 21   C) 22   D) 23   E) 24

6.
4	9		49	81
36	25		x	100

x = ?

A) 110   B) 121   C) 125   D) 225   E) 325

7. 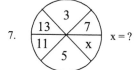 x = ?

A) 14   B) 15   C) 16   D) 17   E) 19

8.  x = ?

A) 54   B) 55   C) 56   D) 58   E) 60

9.

```
     6
  x     5
 24     8
    35
```
x = ?

A) 64   B) 65   C) 66   D) 67   E) 63

10.

```
     2
  x     3
 28     4
    9
```
x = ?

A) 64   B) 65   C) 66   D) 67   E) 68

11.

```
     3
  4     7
  x     10
    17
```
x = ?

A) 18   B) 28   C) 27   D) 37   E) 26

12.  x = ?

   A) 14552   B) 15552   C) 13552   D) 12552   E) 14143

13. 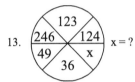 x = ?

   A) 120   B) 140   C) 144   D) 148   E) 150

14.  x = ?

   A) 8   B) 10   C) 12   D) 16   E) 20

15.  x = ?

   A) 72   B) 74   C) 76   D) 78   E) 70

16.  x = ?

A) 53   B) 34   C) 54   D) 56   E) 65

17. 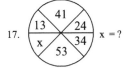 x = ?

A) 37   B) 72   C) 26   D) 77   E) 65

18.  x = ?

A) 61   B) 62   C) 64   D) 68   E) 70

19.  x = ?

A) 88   B) 98   C) 79   D) 69   E) 89

20.  x = ?

A) 10   B) 12   C) 18   D) 20   E) 22

TEST 17

1.  x = ?

   A) 1   B) 2   C) 3   D) 4   E) 5

2.  x = ?

   A) 40   B) 42   C) 43   D) 44   E) 45

3.  x = ?

   A) 3   B) 4   C) 5   D) 6   E) 9

4. x = ?

   A) 83   B) 36   C) 47   D) 30   E) 32

5.

4	12
108	36

x	28
448	112

x = ?

   A) 6   B) 7   C) 10   D) 11   E) 12

6.

2	3
7	5

11	13
x	17

x = ?

A) 19   B) 20   C) 21   D) 22   E) 23

7.

36	40
12	8

44	42
4	x

x = ?

A) 9   B) 10   C) 11   D) 12   E) 6

8.

20	19
4	5

18	22
6	x

x = ?

A) 6   B) 5   C) 4   D) 7   E) 2

9.

24	49
6	13

25	47
7	x

x = ?

A) 10   B) 12   C) 13   D) 11   E) 14

10.

$\sqrt{3}$	3
2	$\sqrt{12}$

6	$6\sqrt{2}$
x	2

x = ?

A) $\sqrt{3}$ B) $2\sqrt{3}$ C) $\sqrt{2}$ D) $2\sqrt{2}$ E) $4\sqrt{2}$

11.
92	41
7	3

82	91
6	x

$x = ?$

A) 6   B) 7   C) 8   D) 9   E) 10

12.
6	8
3	4

5	4
x	8

$x = ?$

A) 5   B) 6   C) 7   D) 8   E) 10

13.
(3 | 4 / 5)   (6 | 8 / 10)   (5 | 12 / x) $x = ?$

A) 10   B) 12   C) 13   D) 16   E) 17

14.
(20 | 7 / 3)   (1 | 7 / 2)   (40 | 24 / x) $x = ?$

A) 4   B) 5   C) 6   D) 7   E) 8

15.
(10 | 12 / 11)   (30 | 12 / 21)   (14 | 12 / x) $x = ?$

A) 10   B) 11   C) 12   D) 13   E) 14

16.   x = ?

A) 1   B) 2   C) 3   D) 4   E) 5

17. x = ?

A) 10   B) 11   C) 12   D) 13   E) 14

18.   x = ?

A) 15   B) 16   C) 17   D) 18   E) 19

19.
6	7	8	14
9	4	14	x

x = ?

A) 18   B) 20   C) 22   D) 24   E) 28

20.
2	5	11	17
3	7	13	x

x = ?

A) 18   B) 19   C) 20   D) 21   E) 23

TEST 18

1.
$\boxed{\begin{array}{c}1\\3\end{array}}$ $\boxed{\begin{array}{c}5\\7\end{array}}$ $\boxed{\begin{array}{c}9\\11\end{array}}$ $\boxed{\begin{array}{c}13\\x\end{array}}$ $x = ?$

A) 14   B) 15   C) 16   D) 17   E) 18

2.
$\boxed{\begin{array}{c}8\\13\end{array}}$ $\boxed{\begin{array}{c}9\\15\end{array}}$ $\boxed{\begin{array}{c}17\\24\end{array}}$ $\boxed{\begin{array}{c}18\\x\end{array}}$ $x = ?$

A) 20   B) 22   C) 24   D) 26   E) 28

3.
$\boxed{\begin{array}{c}10\\13\end{array}}$ $\boxed{\begin{array}{c}17\\21\end{array}}$ $\boxed{\begin{array}{c}15\\20\end{array}}$ $\boxed{\begin{array}{c}20\\x\end{array}}$ $x = ?$

A) 22   B) 23   C) 24   D) 26   E) 27

4.
$\boxed{\begin{array}{c}123\\4\end{array}}$ $\boxed{\begin{array}{c}142\\7\end{array}}$ $\boxed{\begin{array}{c}186\\3\end{array}}$ $\boxed{\begin{array}{c}191\\x\end{array}}$ $x = ?$

A) 10   B) 12   C) 16   D) 17   E) 19

5. $\rightarrow$ x, $\rightarrow$ x, $\rightarrow$ x,y

$\rightarrow$?

A) x_1 B) y   C) x, y   D) x, y, z   E) 2x, y

6. $\rightarrow 360$, $\rightarrow 360$, $\rightarrow$?

A) 340   B) 320   C) 160   D) 180   E) 140

7. $\qquad$, $\qquad$, $\qquad$ + $\qquad$ = ?

y, 2x   2y

A) 2x, 2y   B) y, y   C) 2y, y   D) y, 2y   E) 8x

8. Find the different figure.
   A) ?   B) /   C) +   D) x   E) #

9. Find the different figure.
   A) =   B) ≠   C) ∞   D) %   E) $

10. Find the different figure.
    A) >   B) <   C) =   D) +   E) @

11.

	2	4	6
3	a	2a	3a
4	d	e	4a
5	f	2f	3f

$a + 2f = ?$

A) 20   B) 26   C) 27   D) 30   E) 36

12.

	1	3	5
2	a	b	c
6	b	d	e
5	c	3c	5c

$c + b = ?$

A) 10   B) 18   C) 16   D) 20   E) 25

13.

	4	6	9
12	a	b	-
3	-	-	-
9	-	-	c

$a, b, c = ?$

A) 3, 2, 2   B) 1, 2, 1   C) 3, 2, 1   D) 4, 3, 2   E) 1, 2, 4

14.

	4	6	7
8	a	b	c
9	d	e	b
10	3b	a	2e

$a + b + c = ?$

A) 10   B) 9   C) 8   D) 7   E) 6

15.

	2	3	5
8	a	b	c
9	d	a	e
10	f	q	b

$a + b = ?$

A) 16   B) 14   C) 13   D) 12   E) 11

16.

*	3	4	5
7	20		
8	A	24	
15		B	40

$A + B = ?$

A) 50   B) 53   C) 55   D) 58   E) 60

17.

a	b	c	b	b
c	a	b	a	a
x	y	b	a	b
a	a	c	b	a

$x, y = ?$

A) a, b   B) a, c   C) c, b   D) c, a   E) b, c

18.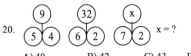

$\triangle \to 7;1, \triangle \to 8;2, \triangle \to ?$

A) 8;3   B) 7;3   C) 9;2   D) 9;1   E) 9;3'

19.

$\triangle \to 18 \quad \square \to 32 \quad \triangle \to ?$

A) 32   B) 31   C) 30   D) 33   E) 34

20.

$x = ?$

(9) (5)(4)   (32) (6)(2)   (x) (7)(2)

A) 40   B) 42   C) 43   D) 44   E) 45

TEST 19

1. 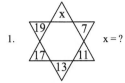 x = ?

A) 21   B) 22   C) 23   D) 27   E) 29

2.  x = ?

A) 1062   B) 1064   C) 1068   D) 1070   E) 1072

3.  x = ?

A) 10   B) 11   C) 12   D) 13   E) 15

4. 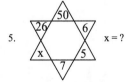 x = ?

A) 30   B) 36   C) 34   D) 32   E) 30

5.  x = ?

A) 36   B) 37   C) 38   D) 40   E) 41

6. 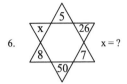   x = ?

   A) 65   B) 64   C) 66   D) 67   E) 68

7. 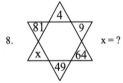   x = ?

   A) 60   B) 62   C) 63   D) 64   E) 65

8. 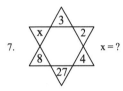   x = ?

   A) 36   B) 34   C) 86   D) 76   E) 72

9.    x = ?

   A) 244   B) 248   C) 252   D) 254   E) 256

10.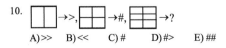
    A) >>   B) <<   C) #   D) #>   E) ##

11. Find the different picture.

A) B) [diagram] C) [diagram] D) [diagram] E) [diagram]

12.

?

A) [diagram] B) [diagram] C) [diagram] D) [diagram] E) [diagram]

13. [> | ≡ | # | >≡ | ?]

A) >< B) ># C) #≡ D) ≡ E) <>

14. [diagram] ?

   I   II   III   IV   V

A) [diagram] B) [diagram] C) [diagram] D) [diagram] E) [diagram]

15. # # # ?

A) # B) # C) # D) # E) #

16.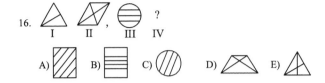

17. ᵃ#ᵦ #ᵇₐ #ᵃₐ ?
   A) #ᵃᵦ   B) ᵃ#ᵦ   C) ₐ#ᵦ   D) ᵃ#ᵦ   E) #ᵃᵦ

18. (figure sequence)
   A)   B)   C)   D)   E)

19.
   3-3-2   4-3-2   ?
   A) 6 - 6 - 2   B) 6 - 6 - 3   C) 5 - 5 - 3
   D) 4 - 5 - 1   E) 5 - 5 - 1

20.
   430   304   ?
   A) 342   B) 346   C) 634   D) 643   E) 372

TEST 20

1. # #ᵇ #ᶜ #→?
   A) #/d B) # C) # D) # E) #

2.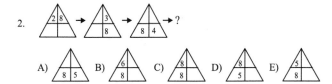

   A) △(8|5) B) △(6|8) C) △(8|8) D) △(8|5) E) △(5|8)

3.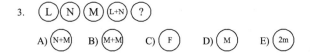
   (L)(N)(M)(L+N)(?)
   A) (N+M) B) (M+M) C) (F) D) (M) E) (2m)

4. ▭→△△, ▯→△,##, ▭→?
   A) 4△   B) 3△   C) 2△,2□   D) 4#   E) 2#

5. Find the different picture.

   A) ◯ B) ▢ C) ▱ D) △ E) ⬡

6. Find the different picture.

I   II

III   IV

A) I   B) II   C) III   D) IV   E) I və II

7.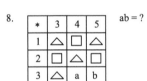

?

A) ◨ B) ◧ C) ▩ D) ▤ E) ▥

8.

*	3	4	5
1	△	□	△
2	□	△	□
3	△	a	b

ab = ?

A) △△   B) □□   C) □△   D) △□   E) △

9.   I   abcde ⎫
     II eabcd ⎪
     III deabc ⎬
     IV ?   ⎭

A) cdeab   B) bcdea   C) bcead   D) abcde   E) cdebb

10.   abc ⎫
      bac ⎬ = ?
      cba ⎭

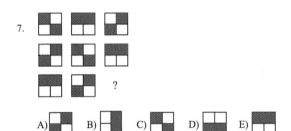

352	453	542	554	543
A) 532	B) 242	C) 452	D) 343	E) 354
235	254	245	354	435

11. →5, →8, →?

   A) 6   B) 7   C) 8   D) 9   E) 10

12. Find the different picture.

   A)   B)   C)   D)   E)

13.

   A)   B)   C)   D)   E)

14.

   A)   B)   C)   D)   E)

15.

   A)   B)   C)

   D)   E)

16.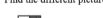

A)   B) C) D) E)

17. Find the different number.
    A) 60 - 70 - 80 - 90   B) 20 - 40 - 60 - 80
    C) 30 - 60 - 90 - 120   D) 40 - 80 - 120 - 160
    E) 10 - 16 - 21 - 28

18.
    16,16,9   16,0,9   ?
    A) 9, 9, 0   B) 9, 0, 9   C) 3, 3, 0
    D) 3, 0, 3   E) 3, 16, 9

19. Find the different picture.

    A)   B)   C)

    D)   E)

20. Find the different picture.

    A)  B) C) D) E)

TEST 21

1.

   A)   B)   C)   D)   E)

2. 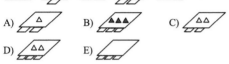 ?

   A)   B)   C)

   D)   E)

3. Find the different picture.

   A)   B)   C)   D)   E)

4. Find the different picture.

   A)   B)   C)   D)   E)

5. Find the different picture.

   A)   B)   C)   D)   E)

6.

5	11	17	?
7	13	19	?

A)
20
21

B)
21
23

C)
23
24

D)
25
26

E)
23
29

7. △△△ → ⊿ , ⌂ →?

A) B) C) D) E)

*	⇒	⇓	⇑	⊔
⇒		26	24	28
⇓		32	30	34
⇑				32

8. ⇑ − ⇒ = ?
A) 1   B) 2   C) 4   D) 6   E) 7

9. ⊔ − ⇓ + ⇑ = ?
A) 12   B) 14   C) 24   D) 16   E) 20

10. ⇒ + ⊔ + ⇑ = ?
A) 36   B) 39   C) 40   D) 42   E) 22

11. $\Rightarrow + \Downarrow + \Uparrow + \sqcup = ?$

    A) 60   B) 58   C) 56   D) 54   E) 52

12.

	⊙*△	x+÷	∨∧⊔
⊙□+	⊙	+	−
x+∨	−	?	∨
∨⊔*	*	−	∨⊔

    A) x+   B) ⊔∨   C) x∨   D) x∨+   E) ∨⊔

13.

    A)   B)   C)   D)   E)

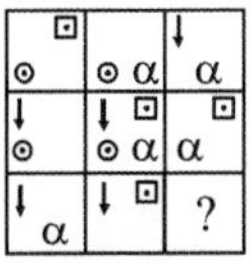

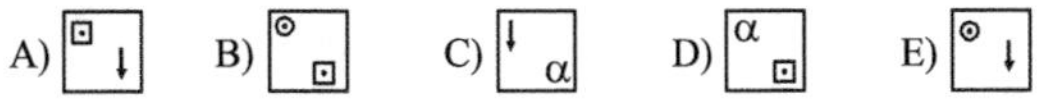

14.

▫	△	◻	⬭
4	6	7	7
6	8	x	y
8		11	11

$x \cdot y = ?$

    A) 81   B) 72   C) 62   D) 52   E) 41

15.

▲	4	5	6
2	14	23	24
3	13	22	23
6	A	B	C

$A + B + C = ?$

    A) 57   B) 67   C) 77   D) 87   E) 97

16.

■	⊙	▲	⊙	⊙
▲	■	⊙	■	■
x	y	⊙	■	⊙
■	■	▲	⊙	■

x, y = ?

A) ■ ⊙   B) ■ △   C) ▲ ⊙

D) ▲ ■   E) ⊙ □

17.

6	3	9
2	4	1
8	9	x

x = ?

A) 6   B) 7   C) 8   D) 9   E) 10

18.

9	7	4
2	7	3
12	13	x

x = ?

A) 7   B) 6   C) 8   D) 9   E) 5

19.

24	7	18
13	8	6
15	6	x

x = ?

A) 9   B) 10   C) 11   D) 12   E) 13

20.

	x	y	z
x		4x	3y
y			
z	6x		9y

x + y - z = ?

A) 3   B) 2   C) 1   D) 0   E) 4

TEST 22

1.

+	x	y	z
x	z+2		16
y			22

$x + z = ?$
A) 10   B) 12   C) 14   D) 16   E) 18

2.

+	m	n
x	13	11
m		10

$\dfrac{m+n}{x} = ?$

A) $\dfrac{7}{10}$ B) $\dfrac{10}{7}$ C) $\dfrac{8}{9}$ D) $\dfrac{9}{8}$ E) $\dfrac{17}{9}$

3.

▲	6	8	10
4	x	6	7
12	9	10	m
14	y	11	12

$x + y + m = ?$
A) 20   B) 22   C) 24   D) 26   E) 28

4.

6	8	4
10	64	6
8	x	3

A) 25   B) 50   C) 75   D) 100   E) 125

5.

∞	8	⧖
⋈	⧗	×
≫	⋀	?

A) ◇   B) ≫   C) ⋀   D) ≪   E) ◇

6.  ?

   A)   B)   C)   D)   E)

7.

   A) 8267   B) 9123   C) 4236   D) 6952   E) 4967

8.

   A)   B)   C)   D)   E)

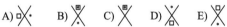

9.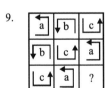

   A)   B)   C)   D)   E)

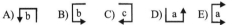

10.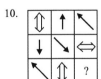

   A) →   B)   C) ↑   D) ↘   E) ←

11.

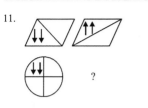

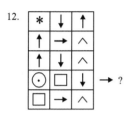   ?

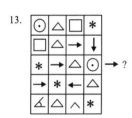

A) B) C) D) E)

12.

*	↓	↑
↑	→	∧
↑	↓	∧
⊙	□	↓
□	→	∧

→ ?

A) 834   B) 214   C) 581   D) 912   E) 234

13.

⊙	△	□	*
□	△	→	↓
*	→	△	⊙
→	*	←	△
∠	△	∧	*

→ ?

A) 6923   B) 3276   C) 7294   D) 0286   E) 9612

14.

A) B) C) D) E)

15.

A) B) C) D) E)

16.

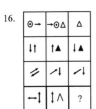

A) ↔↑   B) →△   C) ↕∧   D) ↔∧   E) ▲↓

17.

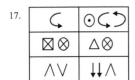

A) ↓↓⊙   B) ∨∧   C) ⊠□   D) ↓↓∨   E) ⊙↺

18.

△	○↓	○↑	↑↓
○↑	○	○↑	↑
○↓	○↓	○	↓
↑↓	↓	↑	?

A) ↓   B) ↑   C) ↑↓   D) ○↑   E) ↑○

19.

→	↓	∨	→	→
∨	→	↓	↓	↓
↓	∨	→	∨	∨
?	?	∨	→	∨

A) →   B) →↓   C) ∨↓   D) ↓↓   E) ⇉

20.

∠	⊔	⊓
⊓	∠	⊔
⊔	⊓	?

A) ∠   B) ⊔   C) ⊓   D) ⊏   E) ⊐

TEST 23

1.

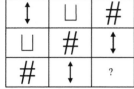

↕	⊔	#
⊔	#	↕
#	↕	?

A) ⊔   B) #   C) ↕   D) ⊓   E) ↑↑

2.

A) ...   B) ...   C) ...   D) ...   E) ...

3. (## ## XX) → 4+4   (XXXX ##) → 8;2

(XXX ##) → ?

A) 3+4   B) 4+6   C) 6+2   D) 6+9   E) 6+10

4.

A) ...   B) ...   C) ...   D) ...   E) ...

5.

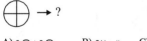

→ *=2#

→ *=⊙+#

→ ?

A) 2⊙+2⊙   B) 2X+#   C) ⊙+2#
D) 2#+4*   E) *+#+⊙

6.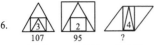

A) 182   B) 192   C) 172   D) 162   E) 152

7.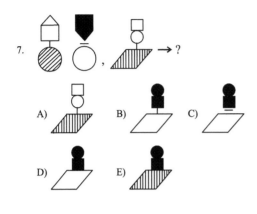

8.
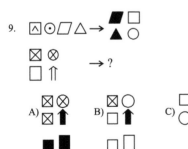

A) 1314   B) 1516   C)1614
D) 2326   E) 2526

9.

A)

B)

C)

D)

E)

10. $x\blacksquare y = x + y - 2$
    $x\blacktriangle y = x - y + 2$
    $x\Delta y = 2 - x + y$
    $(6\blacksquare 2)\Delta(7\blacktriangle 3) = ?$

    A) 2   B) 3   C) 4   D) 5   E) 6

11. $6\triangle4 \to 20$

$3\triangle4 \to 14$

$7\triangle8 \to ?$

A) 10   B) 12   C) 14   D) 15   E) 30

12.

	6	11	4	8
5		16		
7		18		
4	10		8	12
10	16	?	?	?

A) 21, 14, 18   B) –, 14, 18   C) 21, 7, 9

D) –, 7, 9   E) –, –, 9

13.

6	18	8	20
7	21	7	18
3	9	9	22
4	x	12	y

$x + y = ?$

A) 30   B) 36   C) 40   D) 42   E) 50

14.

1	1	5	23
27	3	4	14
8	2	7	47
64	x	y	142

$x + y = ?$

A) 20   B) 22   C) 24   D) 16   E) 30

15.

7	9	8	3,5
8	6	7	4
6	10	8	y
3	7	x	1,5

$x + y = ?$

A) 6   B) 7   C) 8   D) 9   E) 10

16.

12	8	6	4
15	5	8	2
6	10	4	A
9	8	B	3

A + B = ?

A) 20   B) 25   C) 30   D) 36   E) 40

17.

7	5	24
10	15	50
8	9	34
7	7	28
?	?	?

A) 9, 12, 43   B) 10, 12, 25   C) 6, 16, 44   D) 7, 2, 17   E) 6, 7, 27

18.

	2	3	6
4	⊙	⊡	△
1	○	✕	✳
2	a	✳	b

a + b = ?
A) 10   B) 12   C) 14   D) 16   E) 20

19.

	3	4	5
8	△	□	○
9	⊙	△	□
7	□	○	⊠

□ △ ⊙ = ?
A) 4, 5, 7   B) 4, 7, 6   C) 4, 5, 6   D) 7, 5, 3   E) 7, 2, 6

20.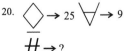

A) 10   B) 12   C) 16   D) 18   E) 20

TEST 24

1. Find the different picture.

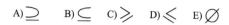

A) ⊇   B) ⊆   C) ⩾   D) ⩽   E) ⦰

2. Find the different picture.

A) |☐   B) ☐| C) ☐̲   D) ☐̄   E) ⊟

3. Find the different number.

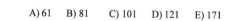

A) 61   B) 81   C) 101   D) 121   E) 171

4.

7	1	x
3	8	22
7	4	22

A) 10   B) 12   C) 14   D) 16   E) 20

5. Find the different picture.

A) ⋁   B) ⊔   C) ⊿   D) ⊆   E) ◎

6.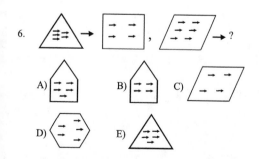

7.

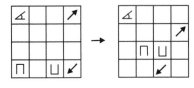

A)∠↙   B)∏■   C)⊔↗   D)↙↗   E)↗∏

8.

+	□	△	*	○
□		16		
△				
*				
○			18	

□x+△*+□○ +△○=?
A) 12   B) 18   C) 20   D) 72   E) 34

9.

A)⊔   B)○   C)∏   D)↙   E)∅

10.

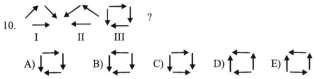

I   II   III

A)↓⟲↓   B)↓⟲↓   C)↓⟲↓   D)↑⟲↑   E)↑⟲↑

11.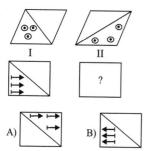

A) 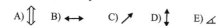 B) C)

D) E)

12. Find the different picture.

A) ⇕ B) ↔ C) ↗ D) ↕ E) ◿

13.

⊙	→	⊙
#	#	↗
→	⊙	→
?	↗	#

A) → B) ↗ C) ⊙ D) # E) ↤

14. Find the different picture.

A) ☐ B) ◉ C) ⊠ D) ✡ E) ✛

15. Find the different picture.

A) ✛ B) ✷ C) ✸ D) ☐ E) ✕

16. Find the different picture.

    A) X   B) ▷   C) ⌂   D) ⊗   E) ⌒

17. Find the different picture.

    A) ⊓   B) 69   C) Ⓥ   D) Ⓧ   E) Ⓥ

18. Find the different picture.

    A) ⌒   B) ↗   C) ♏   D) ⊬   E) ☹

19. Find the different picture.

    A) ☺   B) ⊭   C) X   D) ↰   E) ↳

20. Find the different picture.

    A) →   B) ←   C) ↺   D) ↳   E) ⇉

TEST 25

1. Find the different picture.

   A) ⇉   B) ↑↑   C) ↓↑   D) ⇄   E) ∧

2. Find the different picture.

   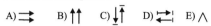

3. Find the different picture.

   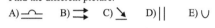

4.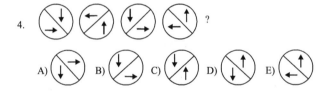

5. Find the different picture.

   A) ▽▽   B) ⇉   C) ⇇   D) || E) ⇄

6. Find the different picture.

   A) ❋   B) ▪▪   C) ✳   D) ⋰•⋰   E) □

7. Find the different picture.

   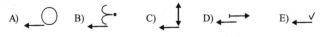

8. Find the different picture.

    A) !!   B)   C) =   D) ?   E) :

9.

    A)   B)   C)   D)   E)

10. Find the different picture.

    A)   B)   C)   D)   E)

11.

    A)   B)   C)   D)    E)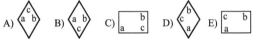

12. 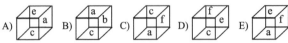 ?

    A)   B)   C)    D) 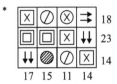   E)

*

X	⊘	⊗	⇉	18
□	□	X	⇊	23
⇊	⊘	⊘	X	14
17	15	11	14	

13. 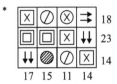 → ?

    A) ⇄   B) ⇊   C) □   D) ⊗   E) ⊘

14. 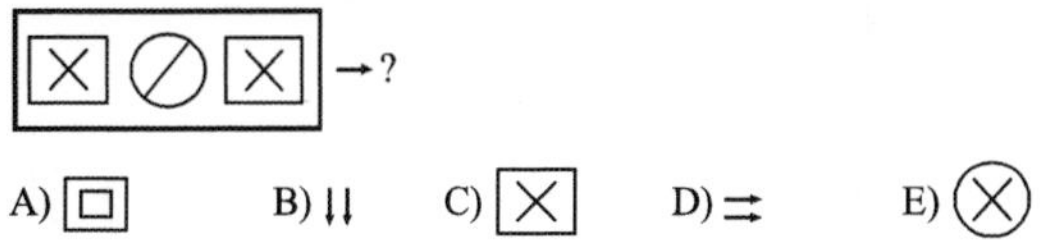 ⊠⊘⊠ → ?

    A) ☐   B) ‖   C) ⊠   D) ⇉   E) ⊗

15. 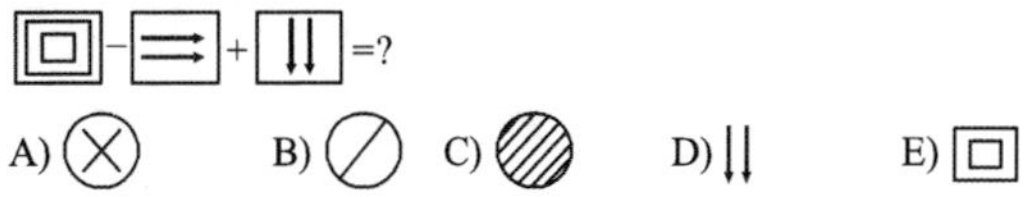 �», - ⇉ + ‖ = ?

    A) ⊗   B) ⊘   C) ◍   D) ‖   E) ◻

16. 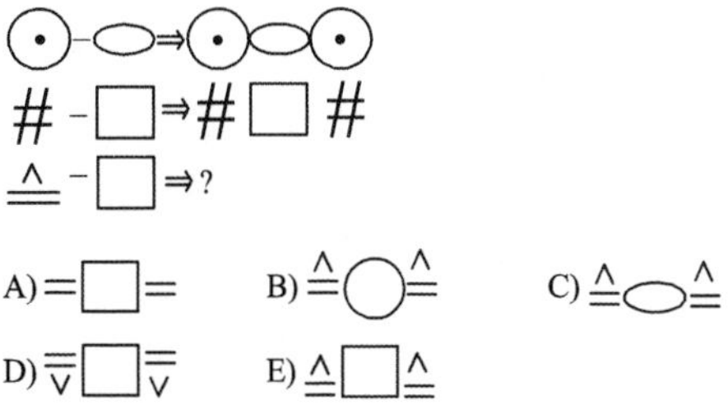 ⊙ - ⊂⊃ ⇒ ⊙ ⊂⊃ ⊙

    # - ☐ ⇒ # ☐ #

    ≙ - ☐ ⇒ ?

    A) =☐=   B) ≙○≙   C) ≙⊂⊃≙

    D) ⩯☐⩯   E) ≙☐≙

17. Find the different picture.
    A) H   B) L   C) K   D) N   E) Z

18. Find the different figure.
    A) ↻   B) ↻   C) ↓   D) ↗   E) ⊟

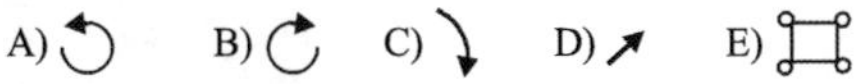

19. Find the different figure.
    A) ⵜ   B) ⇉   C) ‾⋀   D) ↘   E) △

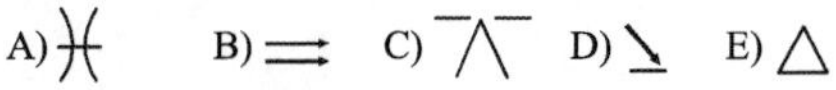

20. Find the different figure.
    A) ⊠   B) ⊘   C) ☑   D) ⊠   E) ⇊

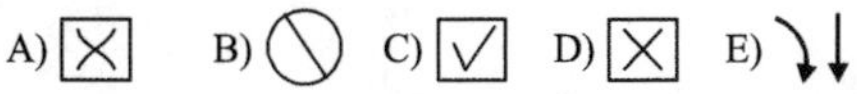

TEST 26

1.

a	b	a	?
b	a	c	?
a	c	d	?
c	d	b	?

A)
b
d
c
a

B)
d
c
a
b

C)
b
d
a
b

D)
c
d
b
a

E)
c
d
a
b

2.
$$\left.\begin{array}{l}12324\\52362\\12725\\82127\\52427\end{array}\right\} \text{ and } 82127 = ?$$

A) $\geq \emptyset \triangle \emptyset \neq$ B) $\blacktriangle \emptyset \neq \emptyset \geq$ C) $\geq \emptyset \blacksquare \bigcirc \emptyset$

D) $\blacktriangle \emptyset \blacksquare \emptyset \triangle$ E) $\square \emptyset \blacktriangle \emptyset \neq$

3.
$$\left.\begin{array}{l}1234\\5243\\6741\\3896\\6435\end{array}\right\} \text{ and } 3896 = ?$$

A) $\neq \blacksquare \square \geq$ B) $\emptyset + \bigcirc \neq$ C) $\blacktriangle \geq \square \emptyset$ D) $\neq \square \emptyset \blacktriangle$ E) $\geq \triangle \emptyset \square$

4.
$$\left.\begin{array}{l}1232\\4567\\2173\\6745\\7321\end{array}\right\} \text{ and } 2173 = ?$$

A) $\blacksquare + \square \emptyset$ B) $\bigcirc \blacksquare \triangle \blacktriangle$ C) $\emptyset \square + \square$

D) $\square \emptyset \blacksquare +$ E) $\triangle \blacktriangle \bigcirc \blacksquare$

5.
$$\left.\begin{array}{l}1212\\3245\\3432\\3465\\1612\end{array}\right\} \text{ and } 3245 = ?$$

A) $\triangle \leftarrow \bigcirc \sqcup$ B) $\triangle \rightarrow \leftarrow \sqcup$ C) $\bigcirc \rightarrow \bigcirc \rightarrow$

D) $\triangle \leftarrow \triangle \rightarrow$ E) $\bigcirc \bigcirc \bigcirc \rightarrow$

6.
$$\left.\begin{array}{l} 1223 \\ 3452 \\ 4167 \\ 7651 \\ 6334 \end{array}\right\}$$
and 7651 = ?

A) ← → → ↑ B) ⊙ ← ⊔ ○ C) ○ = = → D) → ↑ ⊔ = E) ↑ ○ ← ⊙

7.
$$\left.\begin{array}{l} 121 \\ 345 \\ 542 \\ 543 \\ 145 \end{array}\right\}$$
and 145 = ?

A) ↓ → ↓ B) ← ↑ ⊙ C) ⊙ ↑ → D) ⊙ ↑ ← E) ↓ ↑ ⊙

8.
$$\left.\begin{array}{l} 1234 \\ 1254 \\ 6274 \\ 1252 \\ 6238 \end{array}\right\}$$
and 1234 = ?

A) △ □ ▲ ■   B) △ □ ⊙ ■   C) + □ ∅ ■
D) △ □ ⊙ □   E) + □ ▲ ≠

9.
$$\left.\begin{array}{l} 123 \\ 454 \\ 523 \\ 163 \\ 424 \end{array}\right\}$$
and 523 = ?

A) △ □ ▲ B) ■ ○ ■ C) ○ □ ▲ D) △ + ▲   E) ■ □ ■

10.
$$\left.\begin{array}{l} 1232 \\ 4252 \\ 4262 \\ 5762 \\ 8269 \end{array}\right\}$$
and 4252 = ?

A) abcb B) ebfb C) ebhb D) frhb E) mbhn

11. $\left.\begin{array}{l} 12345 \\ 54132 \\ 16725 \\ 56325 \\ 32185 \end{array}\right\}$ and $16725 = ?$

A) abcef   B) feacb   C) ahrbf   D) fhcbf   E) cbamf

12. Find the different figure.

A)   B)   C)   D)   E)

13.

I	II
641	▲ ○ ▲
314	■ ▲ □
233	○ ■ ■
314	■ ▲ □
121	△ □ ▲

$641 = ?$

A) ■ ▲ □   B) ○ ■ ■   C) ■ ▲ □
D) △ □ ▲   E) ▲ ○ ▲

14.

I	II
213	bac
312	cab
123	abc
321	cba
132	acb

and $123 = ?$

A) bac   B) cab   C) abc   D) cba   E) acb

15.

I	II
234	dab
124	acd
224	abd
134	bbd
412	bcd

$431 = ?$

A) bad   B) dca   C) dba   D) dbb   E) dcb

16.

I	II
321	▲ □ △
234	□ ▲ ■
456	■ ○ +
676	+ ∅ +
335	▲ ▲ ○

536 = ?

A) ○ ■ ▲ B) ○ ▲ + C) ▲ □ △
D) ○ + ▲ E) ▲ ○ △

17.
$$\left.\begin{array}{l} 1232 \\ 4215 \\ 4232 \\ 6232 \\ 3174 \end{array}\right\} \text{ and } 4232 = ?$$

A) △ □ ▲ ■   B) □ △ + △   C) ■ △ + △

D) ■ △ □ ○   E) ∅ △ + △

18. Find the different figure.

A)   B) ↑   C) ↺   D) ↷   E) ↶

19. Find the different figure.

A) ∧   B) ∨   C) →   D) ↑   E) ↺

20. Find the different figure.

A) ⌒   B) ↗   C) ⊣⊢   D) △   E) ☺

TEST 27

1. 32⊙24→68
    14⊙31→43
    22⊙24→48
    11⊙77→?
    A) 66   B) 77   C) 88   D) 86   E) 149

2. 15■14→29
    11■15→26
    33■44→?
    A) 66   B) 77   C) 78   D) 87   E) 55

3. 76▲13→17
    84▲15→18
    13▲24→10
    88▲25→?
    A) 20   B) 21   C) 22   D) 23   E) 26

4. 5 ▲1→24
    6 ▲4→20
    3 ▲2→5
    7 ▲5→?
    A) 20   B) 22   C) 23   D) 24   E) 26

5. 64✳21→43
    86✳33→53
    62✳51→11
    98✳44→?
    A) 54   B) 45   C) 56   D) 53   E) 57

6. 21✳32→26
    33✳24→98
    42✳23→86
    41✳23→?
    A) 81   B) 82   C) 83   D) 84   E) 46

7. $84*31 \rightarrow 42$
    $94*22 \rightarrow 50$
    $92*31 \rightarrow 72$
    $82*32 \rightarrow ?$
    A) 20   B) 61   C) 22   D) 23   E) 24

8. $93\Delta \rightarrow 3$
    $42\Delta \rightarrow 2$
    $82\Delta \rightarrow 4$
    $62\Delta \rightarrow ?$
    A) 2   B) 3   C) 4   D) 5   E) 6

9. $21\Delta \rightarrow 4$
    $34\Delta \rightarrow 15$
    $64\Delta \rightarrow 30$
    $73\Delta \rightarrow ?$
    A) 20   B) 22   C) 26   D) 28   E) 30

10. $2\Delta3 \rightarrow 4$
    $3\Delta4 \rightarrow 5$
    $4\Delta5 \rightarrow 6$
    $7\Delta8 \rightarrow ?$
    A) 9   B) 10   C) 11   D) 12   E) 13

11. $1*3 \rightarrow 5$
    $3*5 \rightarrow 7$
    $5*7 \rightarrow 9$
    $7*9 \rightarrow ?$
    A) 11   B) 13   C) 10   D) 12   E) 15

12. $2 \rightarrow 3 \rightarrow 5$
    $7 \rightarrow 11 \rightarrow 13$
    $17 \rightarrow 19 \rightarrow x$
    A) 20   B) 21   C) 22   D) 23   E) 24

13. $2*3 \rightarrow 37$
    $3*4 \rightarrow 145$
    $2*5 \rightarrow 101$
    $3*5 \rightarrow ?$
    A) 246   B) 256   C) 276   D) 226   E) 376

14. $a * b = a + b + 2$
    $a \square b = a + b - 2$
    $(3 * 2) \square (4 * 3) = ?$
    A) 10   B) 12   C) 14   D) 16   E) 20

15. $ab = 12$
    $a + b = 7$
    $a - b = ?,$
    A) 1   B) 2   C) 3   D) 4   E) 5

16. $a + b = 10$
    $ab = 21$
    $a - b = ?$
    A) 2   B) 3   C) 4   D) 5   E) 1

17. $a + b = 14$
    $a \cdot b = 13$
    $a - b = ?$
    A) 10   B) 11   C) 12   D) 13   E) 14

18. $a + b = 11$
    $ab = 24$
    $a - b = ?$
    A) 5   B) 4   C) 3   D) 2   E) 1

19. $a + b = 12$
    $ab = 27$
    $a - b = ?$
    A) 2   B) 3   C) 4   D) 5   E) 6

20.
```
        30
      40  10
    80  40  30
  x  100  60  30
```
    A)100   B) 120   C)160   D)170   E)180

TEST 28

1. X * ⊙
    Λ X V
    X * →
    → X Λ
    V X * → ?
    A) 365   B) 361   C) 837   D) 736   E) 138

2. → ↓ → ⊙ → ?
    ↓ Δ ↓ □
    □ ↓ → V
    ↓ → ⊙ Δ
    Λ → ↓ □
    A) 8346   B) 3437   C) 6431   D) 4375   E) 4546

3. 41, 43, 53, 59, x   x = ?
    A) 60   B) 61   C) 62   D) 64   E) 67

4. 1, 11, 21, 13, 32, 24, x x = ?
    A) 34   B) 33   C) 45   D) 54   E) 47

5. 20, 22, 42, 62, 55, x   x = ?
    A) 75   B) 56   C) 65   D) 74   E) 47

6. 4, 7, 21, 24, 72, x   x = ?
    A) 72   B) 75   C) 80   D) 144   E) 216

7. 2, 5, 10, 17, 26, x   x = ?
    A) 30   B) 32   C) 36   D) 37   E) 39

8. 2, 9, 28, 65, 126, x   x = ?
    A) 210   B) 215   C) 216   D) 217   E) 218

9. aa
    ab
    ba   isə   a + b = ?
    +bb
    ___
    242

    A) 10   B) 11   C) 12   D) 13   E) 14

10. $\dfrac{abc - cba}{ac - ca} = ?$

    A) 10   B) 11   C) 12   D) 13   E) 14

11. 2, 4, 3, 5, 6, 3, 9, 12, 3, 7, 8, x   x = ?
    A) 2   B) 4   C) 5   D) 6   E) 3

12. xyz
    +xzy
    ____ $= ? \Rightarrow x + y + z = ?$
    932

    A) 14   B) 16   C) 12   D) 13   E) 11

13. $12 \to 4$
    $36 \to 12$
    $24 \to 8$
    $72 \to ?$
    A) 20   B) 24   C) 26   D) 25   E) 36

14.   x = ?

    (circle: x, 24, 3, 8, 6, 12, 4, 2)

    A) 1   B) 2   C) 3   D) 4   E) 6

15.

9	12
4	3

12	8
2	3

8	10
5	x

A) 1   B) 2   C) 3   D) 4   E) 5

16.

2	3
7	5

11	13
19	17

23	29
x	31

A) 34   B) 35   C) 36   D) 37   E) 40

17.

A) $\dfrac{3}{4}$ B) $\dfrac{4}{3}$ C) $\dfrac{3}{5}$ D) $\dfrac{3}{7}$ E) $\dfrac{3}{8}$

18.

A) 10   B) 12   C) 15   D) 16   E) 17

19.

→ 10, → 11, → ?

A) 10   B) 11   C) 12   D) 13   E) 14

20.

→ 324, → 248, → ?

A) 600   B) 626   C) 656   D) 556   E) 756

TEST 29

1. ΔΔ
    + ▲▲
    ─────
    77   Δ·▲= ?

    A) 12   B) 13   C) 14   D) 15   E) 16

2. □Δ
    Δ□
    □Δ
    +ΔΠ
    ─────
    110   □·Δ = ?

    A) 5   B) 6   C) 7   D) 8   E) 9

3. ΔΠO
    +OΠΔ
    ─────
    444   ΔΠO = ?

    A) 6   B) 7   C) 8   D) 5   E) 4

4. □·Δ= 72
    □+Δ=17
    □= ?

    A) 9   B) 7   C) 6   D) 5   E) 10

5. □□→4
    ΔΔ→1
    □·Δ→ ?

    A) 1   B) 2   C) 3   D) 4   E) 5

6. □·Δ·O⇒ 6
    □+Δ+O⇒ 6
    O= ?

    A) 3   B) 4   C) 0   D) 5   E) 6

7. $\triangle \cdot \square \cdot \bigcirc = 15$
    $\triangle + \square + \bigcirc = 9$
    $\triangle = ?$

    A) 4   B) 6   C) 5   D) 7   E) 0

8.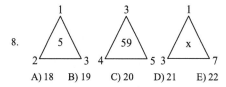

    A) 18   B) 19   C) 20   D) 21   E) 22

9.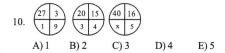

    A) 2   B) 4   C) 5   D) 7   E) 8

10.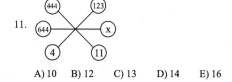

    A) 1   B) 2   C) 3   D) 4   E) 5

11.

    A) 10   B) 12   C) 13   D) 14   E) 16

12. (32)(44)—[22]
    (12)(15)—[7]
    (92)(22)—[x]

    A) 20   B) 21   C) 22   D) 23   E) 25

13.

	5	
3	23	4
	2	

	7	
4	46	6
	3	

	9	
2	x	6
	5	

A) 40   B) 42   C) 44   D) 46   E) 48

14. 3, 4, 7, 6, 9, 7, 10, 12, 7, 15, 14, x   x = ?
A) 3   B) 12   C) 13   D) 66   E) 7

15.

✕	◉	⊞	△
⊕	8	16	8
⊟	4	6	4
⧌	?	?	?

A) 4, 4, 2   B) 4, 8, 2   C) 6, 8, 2   D) 4, 4, 8   E) 8, 4, 2

16.

•	▱	⬡	⌂
▱	14	22	18
⬡	20	32	26
⌂	?	?	?

A) 14, 26, 19   B) 16, 24, 14   C) 19, 24, 12
D) 14, 24, 22   E) 14, 24, 19

17.

	M	N	L
M	8	7	6
N	7	6	5
L	?	?	?

A) 5, 6, 4   B) 4, 6, 5   C) 7, 5, 4   D) 6, 6, 4   E) 6, 5, 4

18.

•	⊠	△	⊕
▯	7	7	11
△	6	6	10
⊕	?	?	?

A) 13, 14, 22   B) 13, 13, 21   C) 14, 14, 22
D) 12, 12, 21   E) 13, 13, 22

19.

•	⊞	⊕	⬡
⊟	8	8	8
⊖	6	6	6
⬡	?	?	?

A) 4, 4, 4,   B) 3, 3, 3   C) 5, 5, 5   D) 9, 9, 9   E) 8, 8, 8

20.

9	7	6	8
1	5	3	1
6	4	5	7
8	3	x	9

A) 1   B) 2   C) 3   D) 4   E) 5

TEST 30

1. V∧✳⊙□
    V↓↑⊙□
    V⊙✳⊙□
    V⊙△↓✳

    V∧✳⊙□ →?

    A) 31297   B)39814   C) 31894   D) 31714   E) 36714

2. ☑ + ☒ + △ = ▢ + △

    ▯ + △̂ + Ⅰ = △̲

    ▯ + ⊔ = ?

    A) △̲ B) △ C) ⊔ D) ▯▯ E) ⊑

3. Find the different picture.

    A) ∪   B) ∩   C) ⩵   D) ⩵   E) $

4. 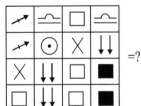 =?

A) 1545	B) 1545	C) 1345	D) 1545	E) 1545
1687	1678	8762	2687	2687
8749	3749	3749	3749	3749
4749	4749	4749	4717	4739

5. Find the different picture.

A)   B) ▢   C) ↑↑   D) ∪   E) ∈

6. Find the different picture.

A) ∉   B) ◇   C) ⊆   D) ⊃   E) ≊

7. Find the different picture.

A) ⊖⊖   B) ▯▯   C) △△   D) ⊆⊇   E) ⌊⌐

8. Find the different picture.

A) ♫   B) ∞   C) ±   D) ≠   E) ∈

9. Find the different picture.

A) ⊆   B) ⊆   C) ⇛   D) ±   E) ≫

10. Find the different picture.

A) ∞   B) π   C) Σ   D) ≥   E) !

11. △ → 360, ▢ → 360, ⌂ → 360, ⬡ → ?

A) 180   B) 360   C) 320   D) 380   E) 270

12.

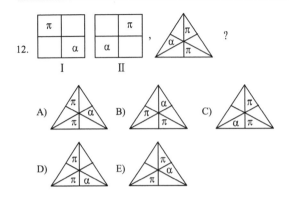

13.

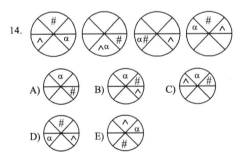

14.

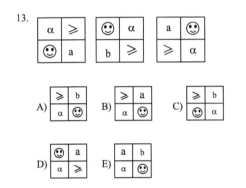

15.

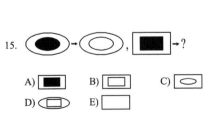

16.

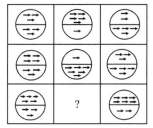

A) 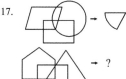 B) C) D) E)

17.

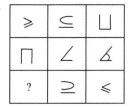

A) △ B) C) D) E)

18.

⩾	⊆	⊔
⊓	∠	◿
?	⊇	⩽

A) B) C) V/ D) U| E)

19. X, ⩾, #, ?

A) B) C) ∈ D) ⩾| E) # =

20. ↑, ↓↓, ≡, ?

A) □ B) ○ C) ▵ D) E) ⊕

TEST 31

1.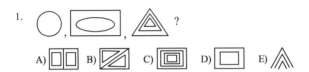

2.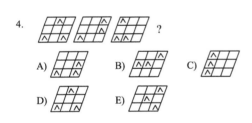

3.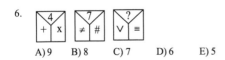

4.

5.

$$\begin{array}{r} \oplus \square \\ + \square \oplus \\ \hline \oplus \oplus \bigcirc \end{array}$$ $\oplus \cdot \square = ?$

A) 6   B) 7   C) 8   D) 9   E) 12

6.

A) 9   B) 8   C) 7   D) 6   E) 5

7.
A) 4   B) 5   C) 6   D) 7   E) 8

8. ⇉△→6, ⊇⊇→4,
⊓⊓→ ?
A) 6   B) 7   C) 8   D) 9   E) 4

9.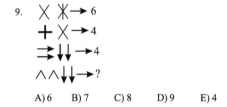
A) 6   B) 7   C) 8   D) 9   E) 4

10.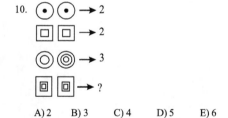
A) 2   B) 3   C) 4   D) 5   E) 6

11.
A) 9   B) 8   C) 12   D) 7   E) 6

12. $7\Delta3 \rightarrow (4,10,22)$

    $6\Delta4 \rightarrow (2,10,25)$

    $3\Delta1 \rightarrow (2,4,4,)$

    $9\Delta2 \rightarrow$???

    A) 7, 10, 19   B) 7, 11, 19   C) 9, 11, 19
    D) 11, 9, 19   E) 11, 12, 18

13. $4 \Rightarrow 9 = 17$

    $6 \Rightarrow 7 = 17$

    $5 \Rightarrow 1 = 10$

    $11 \Rightarrow 7 = ?$

    A) 18   B) 19   C) 20   D) 21   E) 22

14. $14 * 3 = 44$

    $16 * 8 = 32$

    $13 * 9 = 16$

    $15 * 8 = ?$

    A) 20   B) 22   C) 24   D) 26   E) 28

15. $(7\blacktriangle6) = 13$

    $(9\blacktriangle8) = 17$

    $(4\blacksquare3) = 25$

    $(3\blacksquare3) = 18$

    $(6\blacksquare3)\blacktriangle2 = ?$

    A) 2025   B) 2022   C) 2225   D) 2021   E) 2026

16. $7132\otimes = 76$

    $6341\otimes = 184$

    $3355\otimes = 925$

    $6173\otimes = ?$

    A) 617   B) 673   C) 622   D) 621   E) 721

17. $\square$ – ↓↓ → 2

$\diagup\!\!\diagdown$ – ∧ → 2

$\square\!\!\diagup$ – △ → ?

A) 9   B) 8   C) 7   D) 2   E) 3

18. 3□4 → 91

1□5 → 126

2□7 → ?

A) 341   B) 351   C) 331   D) 321   E) 311

19. *246 → 12

■74 → 28

■(*242) → ■15 → 5

*(■49) → ?

A) 9   B) 10   C) 11   D) 12   E) 16

20. 3Δ1 → 8; 26

4Δ2 → 14; 62

4Δ3 → ??

A) 64; 62   B) 60; 64   C) 63; 12
D) 13; 61   E) 63; 64

TEST 32

1. $79*48 = 4$
   $48*24 = 6$
   $25*14 = 2$
   $99*88 = ?$
   A) 1   B) 2   C) 3   D) 4   E) 5

2. $x = ?$

   A) 2   B) 3   C) 4   D) 5   E) 6

3. $(3\square4) \rightarrow 13$
   $(4\square8) \rightarrow 60$
   $(5\square8) \rightarrow 59$
   $(44\square12) \rightarrow ?$
   A) 100   B) 130   C) 140   D) 150   E) 160

4. $423\bullet148 \rightarrow 56$
   $642\bullet436 \rightarrow 120$
   $983\bullet123 \rightarrow ?$
   A) 212   B) 222   C) 232   D) 132   E) 321

5. $8 \Rightarrow 4 = 35$
   $7 \Rightarrow 5 = 35$
   $8 \Rightarrow 2 = 24$
   $9 \Rightarrow 7 = ?$
   A) 64   B) 84   C) 74   D) 94   E) 54

6. $71▲72 → 814$
    $84▲24 → 128$
    $36▲45 → 920$
    $54▲63 → ??$
    A) 9,9   B) 9,19   C) 9,20   D) 20,9   E) 9,18

7. 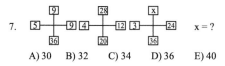   x = ?
    A) 30   B) 32   C) 34   D) 36   E) 40

8.

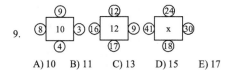

A)160   B) 180   C) 190   D) 210   E) 360

9.

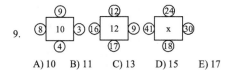

A) 10   B) 11   C) 13   D) 15   E) 17

10.

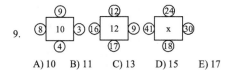

A) 10   B) 12   C) 14   D) 16   E) 18

11.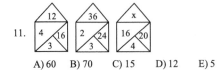

A) 60   B) 70   C) 15   D) 12   E) 5

12.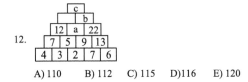

A) 110   B) 112   C) 115   D)116   E) 120

13.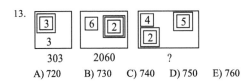

A) 720   B) 730   C) 740   D) 750   E) 760

14.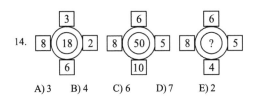

A) 3   B) 4   C) 6   D) 7   E) 2

15.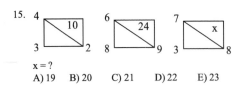

x = ?

A) 19   B) 20   C) 21   D) 22   E) 23

16.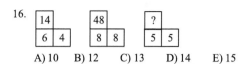

A) 10   B) 12   C) 13   D) 14   E) 15

17.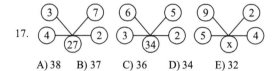

A) 38   B) 37   C) 36   D) 34   E) 32

18.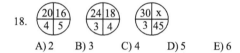

A) 2   B) 3   C) 4   D) 5   E) 6

19.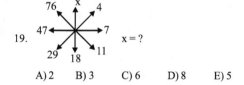

x = ?

A) 2   B) 3   C) 6   D) 8   E) 5

20.

A) 10   B) 11   C) 12   D) 13   E) 14

TEST 33

1. $\boxed{1}\rightarrow 1,$ $\boxed{4}\rightarrow 256,$ $\triangle 2 \rightarrow 8,$

    $\diagup\!\!\boxed{3}\!\diagup\rightarrow ?$

    A) 71   B) 81   C) 84   D) 64   E) 27

2.
$$\begin{array}{cccc}
\textcircled{14} & \textcircled{73} & \textcircled{44} & \textcircled{92} \\
\textcircled{23} & \textcircled{37} & \textcircled{62} & \textcircled{x}
\end{array}$$

    A) 75   B) 76   C) 73   D) 74   E) 78

3.

12	24	18	x	
3	4	6	3	10

    A) 10   B) 20   C) 28   D) 30   E) 32

4.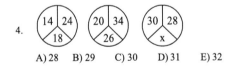

    A) 28   B) 29   C) 30   D) 31   E) 32

5.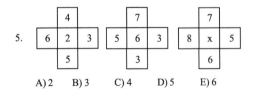

    A) 2   B) 3   C) 4   D) 5   E) 6

6.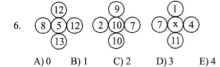

A) 0   B) 1   C) 2   D) 3   E) 4

7.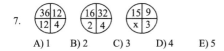

A) 1   B) 2   C) 3   D) 4   E) 5

8.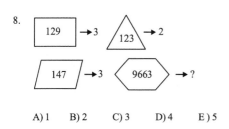

A) 1   B) 2   C) 3   D) 4   E) 5

9. 873 →1   8286 →2

86878 →3   97485 →?

A) 1   B) 2   C) 3   D) 4   E) 5

10.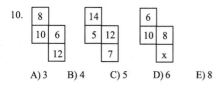

A) 3   B) 4   C) 5   D) 6   E) 8

11. Find the different picture.

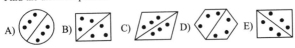

12. Find the different picture.

13.

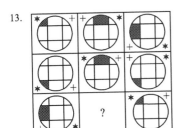

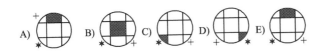

14.

	▲	■	●
▲	16	a	20
✳	12	21	15
■	28	b	35

a, b =?

A) 24, 49   B) 25, 49   C) 28, 49   D) 24, 48   E) 22, 14

15.

2	3	5
7	11	13
17	19	23
29	31	x

x = ?

A) 32   B) 33   C) 34   D) 35   E) 37

16.

2	4	6
3	6	9
2	3	5
4	8	x

$x = ?$

A) 10   B) 12   C) 14   D) 16   E) 9

17.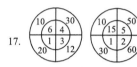

A) 20   B) 21   C) 24   D) 26   E) 28

18. Find the different picture.

A) △   B) └   C) ○   D) ▱   E) ⌂

19.

A) #   B) ≠   C) ||| D) ⫢   E) ⌗

20.

○		○		?	
∧	∨	⇓	⇑	⊂	⊇

A) ⊇   B) ⊆   C) ⊂   D) ≗   E) —

TEST 34

1.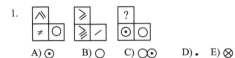

   A) ⊙   B) ○   C) ○⊙   D) ∙   E) ⊗

2.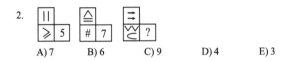

   A) 7   B) 6   C) 9   D) 4   E) 3

3.

   A) 3   B) 4   C) 5   D) 6   E) 7

4.

   A) 2↓   B) 2↑   C) 0   D) ∅   E) ⇊

5. Find the different figure.
   A) ∑   B) π   C) α   D) ∿   E) e

6. Find the different figure.
   A) m   B) n   C) k   D) v   E) α

7. Find the different figure.

A) O⟩─   B) O─⟨   C) →O   D) O←   E) ⇒O

8. $8▲4 → 3$

$9▲2 → \dfrac{11}{7}$

$10▲8 → 9$

$24▲4 → ?$

A) $\dfrac{5}{7}$ B) $\dfrac{7}{5}$ C) $\dfrac{6}{5}$ D) $\dfrac{5}{6}$ E) $\dfrac{1}{3}$

9. Find the different picture.
A) ⋊   B) ⊬   C) ⊓   D) ℽ   E) ⊠

10. Find the different figure.
A) K   B) M   C) N   D) F   E) Y

11.  → ?

A) ◖   B) ⊕   C) ⊠   D) ◭   E) ◓

12. 6, 7, 8, 9, x, 63, 48, 35
   A) 81   B) 80   C) 82   D) 79   E) 78

13. $6 → A, 7 → Y, 9 → D, 4 → ?$
   A) A   B) C   C) D   D) E   E) İ

14.

A) ⬡ B) ⬡ C) ⬡ D) ⬡ E) △

15.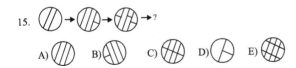

A) ⊘ B) ⊘ C) ⊕ D) ⊘ E) ⊞

16.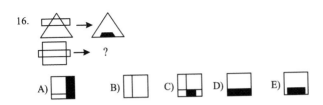

A) ▢ B) ▢ C) ▢ D) ▢ E) ▢

17. 3421 → 12; 2
    7284 → 14; 32
    6221 → ?
    A) 12; 3   B) 12; 21   C) 12; 2   D) 13; 3   E) 12; 7

18. 7514 → 7
    6213 → 4
    7436 → ?
    A) 5   B) 6   C) 2   D) 8   E) 9

19. 6543 → 11; 7
    2175 → 3; 12
    6431 → ?; ?
    A) 4; 10   B) 5; 11   C) 10; 4   D) 11; 5   E) 12; 6

x	4	6	8	10
y	4	8	11	13
z	5	9	12	14

20. x = 12   y = ?
    A) 10   B) 11   C) 12   D) 13   E) 14

TEST 35

1.

*	3462	965	9562
123	32		2
24	24		2
18		?	

A)2　　　　B)5　　　　C) 42　　　　D)6　　　　E) –

2. $a \boxtimes b = \dfrac{a^2 + b^2}{3}$

$a \blacktriangle b = \dfrac{ab}{3}$

$(3 \boxtimes 2) \blacktriangle (3 \blacktriangle 1)$

A) $\dfrac{9}{14}$　　　B) $\dfrac{3}{14}$　　　C) $\dfrac{14}{6}$　　　D) $\dfrac{14}{9}$　　　E) $\dfrac{14}{5}$

3.

A) 　　B) 　　C) 　　D) 　　E)

4. Find the different picture.

A) 　　B) 　　C) 　　D) 　　E)

5. 8, 12, 10, 14, 12, 16, x　　x = ?

A)12　　B) 13　　C)14　　D) 16　　E) 15

6. 7, 64, 8, 81, 9, 100, 10, x　　x =?

A) 110　　B) 121　　C) 131　　D) 141　　E) 161

7.
$$\left.\begin{array}{l} 123 \\ 344 \\ 225 \\ 551 \\ 115 \end{array}\right\} \begin{array}{l} abc \\ cdd \\ bbe \\ eea \\ aae \end{array} \quad bbe = ?$$

A) 115   B) 551   C) 225   D) 344   E) 123

8.
$$\left.\begin{array}{l} 834 \\ 214 \\ 581 \\ 912 \\ 234 \end{array}\right\} \text{ and } \quad 581 = ?$$

A) ■ ○ △   B) ⊙ ▢ △   C) ▲ ■ ▢   D) ● ▢ ⊙   E) ⊙ ○ △

9.
$$\left.\begin{array}{l} abcd \\ efqa \\ dfha \\ bamf \\ hfbn \end{array}\right\} \text{ and } \quad bamf = ?$$

A) 4187   B) 5824   C) 7834   D) 1498   E) 3816

10. (20)(17) → (148)

(12)(13) → (100)

(15)(25) → (?)

A) 100   B) 110   C) 115   D) 120   E) 160

11.

+ ✳ α ⊙	☒▢▲	V∧⊙	⊙✳ →
+ ⊙ x =	▲▲▢	# ∧V	⊙✳↑
α =	☒	⊀⊙	?

A) →   B) ↑   C) →↑   D) ⇒   E) ✳✳

188

12.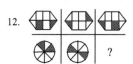

A)    B)    C)    D)    E)

13.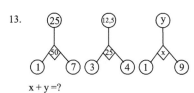

x + y = ?

A) 100   B) 101   C) 102   D) 123   E) 106

14.

6	4	4	20
6	8	20	28
7	3	7	14
5	3	2	x

A) 10   B) 11   C) 12   D) 13   E) 14

15.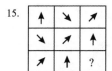

A) ↗   B) ↘   C) ↖   D) ↑   E) ↓

16.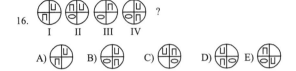

    I   II   III   IV

17.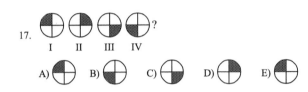

    I   II   III   IV

18. ⊡ ⊔⊓⊙ → ⊕ ⩾ ≠ ▲
    ▲ ≠ ⊕ ⩾   ⊙⊓⊔ ⊡

    abcd → ?
    efkm

    A) kmfe   B) kmfe   C) efkm   D) efkm   E) kmfa
       cdba   dcba   cdba   dbac   dbac

19. ⊔⊓⊙
    ⊙⊔ △
    ⊔⊓ ⊡
    ⊡⊔⊙
    △⊔⊓→?

    A) 123   B) 415   C) 126   D) 614   E) 712

20. ⊔⊓⊔○
    ⊓⊙⊓ △
    △⊓⊔ ▲
    ⊓⊔○⊙
    ⊡⊔⊓ △

    ⊔⊓⊔○ →?

    A) 1213   B) 2425   C) 5216   D) 2134   E) 7125

TEST 36

1.

a	b	c	b
a	d	e	f
e	f	c	L
c	f	c	L

= ?

A) 1252　　B) 3252　　C) 1252　　D) 5657　　E) 1352
　　1346　　　　1336　　　　1346　　　　7546　　　　1446
　　4556　　　　4657　　　　4657　　　　1346　　　　4657
　　5657　　　　5657　　　　5657　　　　1252　　　　5657

2.

a	b	d	c
a	b	d	e
f	m	e	a
m	L	b	d
f	m	b	d

= ?

A) 1257　　B) 1257　　C) 1247　　D) 2157　　E) 3425
　　1246　　　　1256　　　　1256　　　　2156　　　　3825
　　3451　　　　3461　　　　1634　　　　3461　　　　3461
　　4825　　　　4825　　　　5248　　　　4825　　　　1261
　　3425　　　　3425　　　　3425　　　　3425　　　　1257

3. $6436 \rightarrow 6$
   $7231 \rightarrow 11$
   $9343 \rightarrow 15$
   $8452 \rightarrow ?$
   A) 20　　B) 21　　C) 22　　D) 23　　E) 25

4. $1231 \rightarrow 43$
   $3624 \rightarrow 60$
   $2915 \rightarrow 44$
   $6514 \rightarrow ?$
   A) 70　　B) 72　　C) 73　　D) 75　　E) 79

5. $12\square10 \rightarrow 6,5,4$
   $16\square6 \rightarrow 8,3,100$
   $18\square4 \rightarrow 9,2,196$
   $8\square6 \rightarrow ???$
   A) 4, 3, 36　　　　B) 4, 3, 64　　　C) 4, 3, 32
   D) 4, 3, 16　　　　E) 4, 3, 4

6.

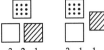

3 - 2 - 1   3 - 1 - 1 - 1

 → ?

A) 4 - 1 - 2 - 1   B) 4 - 1 - 1 - 1 - 2   C) 4 - 2 - 2 - 1
D) 3 - 2 - 1 - 1   E) 4 - 2 -2 - 2

7.

3 - 1 - 1 - 1   5 - 2 - 2 - 1

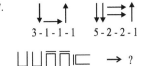 → ?

A) 5 - 2 - 1 - 1   B) 5 - 2 - 2 - 1   C) 4 - 2 - 1 - 1
D) 4 - 2 - 1 - 1   E) 3 - 2 - 1 - 1

8. △ ≥ L → 332

□ ⊓ △ → 443

⊘ ⊓ ⊏ → ?

A) 433   B) 533   C) 233   D) 544   E) 522

9. Find the different picture.

A) ⊔⊔   B) ↑↑   C) ↕↕   D) ⩚   E) ⊙⊙

10. Find the different picture.

A) ◸◹   B) ⊘⊘   C) ◺◹
D) ▱▱   E) ∨∧

11. Find the different picture.

A) ⬭   B) ▭   C) ⊐   D) ◯   E) ⬡

12. Find the different picture.

13. Find the different picture.

14. Find the different picture.

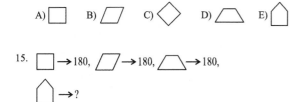

15.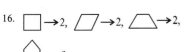

A) 180   B) 360   C) 540   D) 580   E) 380

16. □→2, ⟋⟋→2, △→2,

◠→?

A) 2   B) 3   C) 4   D) 5   E) 6

17. Find the different picture.

18. □□☑☒☒→?
    □○○☒☒
    □☒☑☒☒
    □☒○○☒
    □☒⊕○☑

A) 92105   B) 90723   C) 92703   D) 92523   E) 97523

19.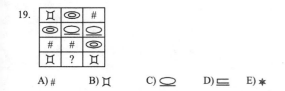

A) #   B) ☒   C) ⊖   D) ⊑   E) ✳

20. Find the different number.
    A) 34   B) 51   C) 68   D) 17   E) 72

TEST 37

1.

   A) 100   B) 113   C) 106   D) 108   E) 110

2.

3	6	3	5
7	21	24	x	7
4	8	7	2

   x = ?

   A) 16   B) 17   C) 18   D) 19   E) 20

3.

+	x	y	z
x		12	
y			18
z	16		

   x + y + z = ?

   A) 20   B) 21   C) 22   D) 23   E) 24

4.

⊙	4	6	8
1		12	
3			48
4			

▲	6	8	10
4		16	
5			25
6			

   (9⊙2)⊙(6▲2)=?

   A) 422   B) 442   C) 452   D) 462   E) 432

5.

$$\left.\begin{array}{l} 21436 \\ 45858 \\ 23658 \\ 25456 \\ 65458 \end{array}\right\} \Rightarrow 65458 = ?$$

   A) 56367   B) 83517   C) 61717
   D) 84635   E) 81615

6. □⊙✳△□■✳△□⊙⊀ ✳↓⊙⊗⊕ ?

    A) □   B) △   C) ■   D) ⊀   E) ✳

7. $$\frac{\begin{array}{c}A\\+B\end{array}}{16} \quad \frac{\begin{array}{c}C\\+A\end{array}}{9} \quad \Rightarrow \quad \frac{\begin{array}{c}B\\-C\end{array}}{?}$$

    A) 6   B) 7   C) 8   D) 9   E) 5

8. $$\frac{\begin{array}{c}ab\\ba\\+ba\end{array}}{180} \quad a \cdot b = ?$$

    A) 8   B) 9   C) 6   D) 3   E) 4

9. $a \odot b = a^2 - b$

    $a \triangle b = a + b^2$

    $a \bullet b = a + b$

    $(6 \odot 4) \triangle (7 \bullet 3)$

    A) 136   B) 132   C) 142   D) 152   E) 160

10. $6 \odot 5 \rightarrow 11$

    $7 \odot 6 \rightarrow 13$

    $7 \odot 4 \rightarrow 33$

    $6 \odot 2 \rightarrow ?$

    A) 28   B) 30   C) 32   D) 34   E) 36

11. $4321 \rightarrow 4$

    $56213 \rightarrow 5$

    $121122 \rightarrow 6$

    $333 \rightarrow ?$

    A) 3   B) 2   C) 4   D) 5   E) 6

12. $60\blacksquare12 \rightarrow 24$

$18\blacksquare24 \rightarrow 14$

$72\blacksquare21 \rightarrow 31$

$27\blacksquare72 \rightarrow ?$

A) 28   B) 27   C) 24   D) 30   E) 33

13. $\blacksquare(\oslash\otimes\sqcup\sqcap) \rightarrow \sqcup\sqcap\oslash\otimes$

$\blacktriangle(xyz\tau) \rightarrow yx\tau z$

$\blacksquare(\blacktriangle6897) \rightarrow ?$

A) 8674   B) 6976   C) 7986   D) 8679   E) 8476

14. I $24\blacksquare(8\blacksquare4) = 12$

II $(24\blacksquare2)\blacksquare(9\blacksquare3) = 4$

$128\blacksquare(96\blacksquare(36\blacksquare6)) = ?$

A) 12   B) 11   C) 10   D) 9   E) 8

15. I   3   6   30   240

II   3   9   54   576

III   4   16   ?   ?

A) 54, 662   B) 56, 672   C) 56, 642

D) 48, 672   E) 58, 632

16. 12   4   40

16   3   65

17   12   ?

A) 20   B) 23   C) 24   D) 26   E) 25

17.

24	48	77
	4	

30	60	96
	5	

72	36	x
	y	

x · y = ?

A) 222   B) 333   C) 444   D) 324   E) 224

18.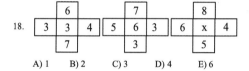

A) 1   B) 2   C) 3   D) 4   E) 6

19.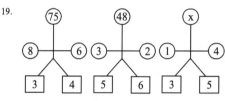

x = ?

A) 10   B) 11   C) 17   D) 18   E) 20

20.

A
1	2	4	3
4	1	2	3
4	3	2	1

=

B
?	≠	⊙	✳
⊙	?	≠	✳
⊙	✳	?	→

A) → ⊙ ≠   B) → → ≠   C) ≠ → →
D) → → ⊙   E) → → ≠ ⊙

TEST 38

1. Find the different picture.

    A) △|○ B) □|⊨ C) ◇∛◇ D) ⇒∛○ E) ⇒∛◇
       ⊔|□   ○|▽   ○   ◇   △

2.
    (⊔∈⊔) (# #) (⊔∈∈)
     ⇒   ∈ ∈   #
           ⇒

    3, 2, 3, 0   0, 3, 2, 3   ?

    A) 3, 2, 2, 1   B) 2, 3, 2, 2   C) 0, 2, 3, 3
    D) 2, 1, 2, 3   E) 3, 2, 3, 2

3.   ⊙ ✡   ✡   ✡   ?

    A) ✡   B) ✡   C) ✡   D) ✡   E) ✡

4.   (⊞)→(⊞) ; (‖) ?

    A) (\\)   B) (‖)   C) (⊔)   D) (/)   E) (⊆)

5.
    | ⊆ | ∈ | ↓ | ⊔ |
    | ⩾ | ⊄ | ? | ∅ |
    | ↓ | ⊄ | ∈ | ⊆ |
    | ⊔ | ⊐ | ⩾ | ⊐ |

    A) ∅   B) ⊔   C) ⊐   D) ⊘   E) ↓

6.

A) ○   B) ⩾   C) ⊗   D) ⊕   E) △

7.

A) ⊐   B) ⊸   C) ↓   D) ↑   E) ⩾

8.

x = ?

A) 10   B) 11   C) 12   D) 13   E) 9

9.

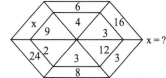

x = ?

A) 2   B) 3   C) 4   D) 5   E) 6

10.

abc
abc
+abc
—————
402

a · b · c = ?

A) 10   B) 13   C) 14   D) 12   E) 16

11. $6 \otimes 4 \rightarrow 18$
    $3 \otimes 5 \rightarrow 14$
    $9 \otimes 2 \rightarrow 20$
    $3 \otimes 12 \rightarrow ?$
    A) 20   B) 22   C) 24   D) 28   E) 30

12. aa $a + b + c = ?$
    bb
    +cc
    ———
    143
    A) 10   B) 11   C) 12 D) 13   E) 14

13. $64 \odot 22 \rightarrow 14$
    $33 \odot 17 \rightarrow 14$
    $21 \odot 20 \rightarrow 5$
    $64 \odot 10 \rightarrow ?$
    A) 10   B) 11   C) 13   D) 14   E) 12

14. $23 \square 15 \rightarrow 5, 6, 38$
    $42 \square 24 \rightarrow 6, 6, 66$
    $15 \square 27 \rightarrow ???$
    A) 6, 9, 52   B) 6, 9, 42   C) 6, 9, 32
    D) 5, 14, 43   E) 6, 9, 22

15. $24 \boxtimes \rightarrow 18$, $19 \boxtimes \rightarrow 30$
    $60 \blacktriangle \rightarrow 21$, $12 \blacktriangle \rightarrow 5$
    $72 \blacktriangle \boxtimes \rightarrow ?$
    A) 21   B) 22   C) 23   D) 24   E) 27

16. 4, 8, 32, 36, 144, ?
    A)146   B) 148   C) 152   D) 288   E) 256

17. **I**   **II**
     80   1
     40   4
     20   9
     10   16
     ?   ?
    A) 5, 17   B) 5, 20   C) 5, 24   D) 5, 25   E) 5, 26

18. **I**   6   2   32
    II   5   3   16
    III 7   4   ?
    A) 33   B) 23   C) 24   D) 32   E) 30

19.

    A) 300   B) 310   C) 316   D) 318   E) 320

20.

    A) 120   B) 122   C) 23   D) 125   E) 124

TEST 39

1.

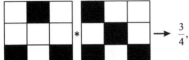 $\rightarrow \dfrac{3}{4}$,

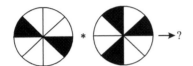 $\rightarrow$?

A) $\dfrac{3}{2}$ B) $\dfrac{1}{3}$ C) $\dfrac{2}{3}$ D) 1   E) $\dfrac{4}{3}$

2.

a a	a a b	a|b a|b
b / a a	b|a b|a	a a b b b
a|b a|b	b b b a a	?

A) $\dfrac{a}{bbbb}$ B) b b b b \| a a   C) $\dfrac{a}{b}$ D) b\|a b\|a   E) b b b b \| a a

3.

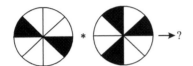 $\rightarrow$?

A)   B)   C)

D)   E)

4.

I

II

A)   B)   C)   D)   E)

5.

A) Ⓐ   B) △ⱥ   C) [a]   D) [b]   E) [c]

6.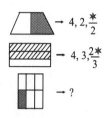

→ 4, 2, $\frac{*}{2}$

→ 4, 3, $\frac{2*}{3}$

→ ?

A) 6, 4, $\frac{*}{6}$ B) 4, 6, 2*   C) 4, 6, $\frac{*}{6}$

D) 3, 4, $\frac{*}{6}$ E) $\frac{*}{6}$, 4, 6

7. ↓⊙△△⊙□≠△⊙△≠≠□ ?
   A) ↓   B) △   C) ≠   D) □   E) ⊙

8. □↓○□↕*≠△↓⊙⊗⊙ ?
   A) ↓   B) □   C) ≠   D) ⊙   E) ↑

9.
↓↑→←□
↑←→↓□
↓↑⊙↓○   } ise ↓↑⊙↓○ = ?
●←↑←□
⊙←→←○

A) 64347   B) 84245   C) 12617
D) 24315   E) 12345

10. ▲▼▼▼▼▼→ 4

▼▼▼▲→ 4

▲▼▼▼▼▼▲→ 5

•[•▼▼▼▼▼▼] → ?

A) 6   B) 5   C) 4   D) 3   E) 7

11. 7Δ2 → 5

8Δ7 → 41

6Δ2 → 4

9Δ8 → ?

A) 55   B) 65   C) 45   D) 35   E) 75

12. 1, 2, 4, 3, 6, 36, 7, 14, ?
    A) 186   B) 196   C) 197   D) 200   E) 173

13. 8, 4, 25, 6, 3, 16, 10, 5, 36, 14, 7, ?
    A) 60   B) 62   C) 64   D) 46   E) 73

14.   ab
        ab
      $\dfrac{+ab}{222}$ $a + b = ?$

    A) 10   B) 11   C) 12   D) 8   E) 9

15.

a	c	b
b	a	c
c	b	a
c	b	a
a	c	b
b	a	c
b	a	
c	b	?
a	c	

A) b   B) a   C) c   D) b   E) c
   a   b   b   c   a
   c   c   a   a   b

16.
$$\begin{array}{r} ab \\ ab \\ ba \\ +ba \\ \hline 110 \end{array} \quad \frac{a+b}{a\cdot b} = ?$$

A) $\dfrac{5}{4}$ B) $\dfrac{5}{6}$ C) $\dfrac{6}{5}$ D) $\dfrac{5}{7}$ E) $\dfrac{5}{8}$

17. 4, 8, 2, 10, 12, 3, 14, 16, 5, 18, 20, ?

A) 7   B) 9   C) 13   D) 11   E) 15

18.

A) ⊕   B) ⊗   C) ☒   D) ÷   E) /π\

19.

$\left(\dfrac{2}{3}\right)\left(\dfrac{3}{5}\right)\left(\dfrac{7}{5}\right)\left(\dfrac{11}{7}\right)$?

A) $\left(\dfrac{11}{13}\right)$ B) $\left(\dfrac{11}{14}\right)$ C) $\left(\dfrac{13}{11}\right)$ D) $\left(\dfrac{11}{9}\right)$ E) $\left(\dfrac{10}{11}\right)$

20. $\boxed{5\ \ 7}$ $\boxed{7 \atop 11}$ $\boxed{13\ 11}$?

A) $\boxed{15 \atop 13}$ B) $\boxed{14 \atop 13}$ C) $\boxed{16 \atop 13}$ D) $\boxed{17 \atop 13}$ E) $\boxed{17\ 13}$

TEST 40

1.
$$\left.\begin{array}{l}\text{▲▲○} \\ \text{⊙□○} \\ \text{⊙◫□} \\ \text{▲◿▲} \\ \text{□⊙□}\end{array}\right\} = ?$$

A) 663	B) 633	C) 633	D) 633	E) 773
823	823	723	623	723
852	852	852	852	852
646	646	646	646	646
283	282	282	283	282

2.
$$\left.\begin{array}{l}\text{▨▨▲} \\ \text{▲▨▨} \\ \text{⊙○○} \\ \text{□□▲} \\ \text{⊞⊞⊙}\end{array}\right\} \left\{\begin{array}{l}008 \\ 226 \\ 883 \\ 655 \\ 556\end{array}\right. \quad \text{if } \square\square\text{▲} = ?$$

A) 008   B) 226   C) 883   D) 655   E) 556

3.
$$\left.\begin{array}{l}321 \\ 923 \\ 988 \\ 799 \\ 332\end{array}\right\} \Rightarrow ?$$

A) ○□△   B) ○△□   C) ○□△   D) ○□△   E) ○□△
  ⊕□○   ⊕□○   ⊕□□   ⊕□○   ○○□
  ⊕○⊙   ⊕○⊙   ⊕○△   ○○○   ⊕⊕■
  ■⊕⊕   □⊕⊕   ■⊕⊕   ■⊕⊕   ⊕○⊙
  ○○□   ○○□   ○○□   ○○□   ○□△

4.
$$\left.\begin{array}{l}\text{□△⊙} \\ \text{■⊞○} \\ \text{▲■△} \\ \text{◿◿⊙} \\ \text{▨▨△}\end{array}\right\} \left\{\begin{array}{l}551 \\ 448 \\ 671 \\ 703 \\ 218\end{array}\right. \quad \text{if } \text{▲■△} = ?$$

A) 551   B) 448   C) 218   D) 671   E) 703

5.
$$\left.\begin{array}{l}\text{⊙⊙⊞} \\ \text{△▲○} \\ \text{□△▲} \\ \text{□□⊙} \\ \text{△■■}\end{array}\right\} \left\{\begin{array}{l}880 \\ 177 \\ 228 \\ 163 \\ 216\end{array}\right. \quad \text{if } \text{□△▲} = ?$$

A) 880   B) 177   C) 228   D) 163   E) 216

6.

△□○ → 123
○□△ → 321
▲■△ → 886   if   ▲■△ = ?
▲○□ → 632
⊙○▲ → 671

A) 123   B) 321   C) 886   D) 632   E) 671

7.

⊙⊞⊞ → 800
⊙□□ → 361
▲▲△ → 773   if   ○▲△ = ?
■■○ → 661
○▲△ → 822

A) 800   B) 361   C) 773   D) 661   E) 822

8.

⊙⊙⊞ → 761
□■○ → 883
○○⊞ → 330   if   ■△△ = ?
⊙⊙○ → 273
■▲△ → 880

A) 880   B) 273   C) 330   D) 883   E) 761

9.

⊕⊕⊙ → 776
⊙⊕⊕ → 821
△□⊞ → 120   if   ○□△ = ?
⊙□△ → 899
■■▲ → 998

A) 776   B) 821   C) 120   D) 899   E) 998

10.

△□⊞ → 881
□○⊞ → 763
▲■○ → 673   if   ▲■○ = ?
■▲○ → 230
⊙○△ → 120

A) 881   B) 763   C) 673   D) 230   E) 120

11.
$$\left.\begin{array}{l} \triangle\,\square \\ \square\,\triangle \\ \bigcirc\,\blacktriangle \\ \blacktriangle\,\blacktriangle \\ \odot\,\square \end{array}\right\} \left\{\begin{array}{l} 12 \\ 21 \\ 36 \\ 66 \\ 82 \end{array}\right.$$ if $\triangle\,\square\,\odot\,\blacktriangle = ?$

A) 1233   B) 1246   C) 1286   D) 1276   E) 1386

12.
$$\left.\begin{array}{l} \oplus\,\oplus \\ \odot\,\triangle \\ \square\,\triangle \\ \bigcirc\,\boxplus \\ \triangle\,\odot \end{array}\right\} \left\{\begin{array}{l} 99 \\ 18 \\ 30 \\ 21 \\ 81 \end{array}\right.$$ if $\oplus\,\triangle\,\square\,\odot = ?$

A) 9132   B) 9156   C) 9128   D) 9148   E) 9158

13.
$$\left.\begin{array}{l} \oplus\,\oplus \\ \blacktriangle\,\blacktriangle \\ \square\,\triangle \\ \triangle\,\odot \\ \blacksquare\,\triangle \end{array}\right\} \left\{\begin{array}{l} 71 \\ 78 \\ 21 \\ 66 \\ 99 \end{array}\right.$$ if $\triangle\,\blacktriangle\,\odot\,\blacktriangle = ?$

A) 4689   B) 1687   C) 4684   D) 4682   E) 4827

14.
$$\left.\begin{array}{l} \square\,\square \\ \odot\,\triangle \\ \triangle\,\odot \\ \blacksquare\,\square \\ \blacktriangle\,\triangle \end{array}\right\} \left\{\begin{array}{l} 22 \\ 81 \\ 18 \\ 72 \\ 61 \end{array}\right.$$ if $\odot\,\triangle\,\blacksquare\,\square = ?$

A) 8172   B) 8173   C) 8174   D) 2718   E) 2728

15.
$$\left.\begin{array}{l} \blacksquare\,\blacksquare \\ \square\,\blacksquare \\ \triangle\,\blacktriangle \\ \blacktriangle\,\triangle \\ \square\,\bigcirc \end{array}\right\} \left\{\begin{array}{l} 23 \\ 61 \\ 16 \\ 27 \\ 77 \end{array}\right.$$ if $\bigcirc\,\square\,\blacksquare = ?$

A) 327   B) 723   C) 347   D) 743   E) 527

16. ↓↑ ⎫   ⎧ 12
     ⊙⊙ ⎪   ⎪ 11
     ⊠→ ⎬   ⎨ 33   if ↓ = ?
     →⊠ ⎪   ⎪ 46
     ↑↓ ⎭   ⎩ 64

A) 1   B) 2   C) 3   D) 4   E) 5

17. ↓↓⊙ ⎫   ⎧ 639
     ⊠⊠⊙ ⎪   ⎪ 399
     ↑↑↓ ⎬   ⎨ 221   if ↑↑↓ = ?
     ⊙●● ⎪   ⎪ 443
     →⊙● ⎭   ⎩ 113

A) 639   B) 399   C) 221   D) 113   E) 443

18. ●⊙↑ ⎫   ⎧ 932
     ↑⊙● ⎪   ⎪ 239
     ↑↑→ ⎬   ⎨ 226   if ●↓↑⊙ = ?
     →↓↓ ⎪   ⎪ 611
     ↑↓↓ ⎭   ⎩ 211

A) 9123   B) 9124   C) 1923   D) 1932   E) 1942

19. ↓→↑ ⎫   ⎧ 565
     ⊙→↓ ⎪   ⎪ 474
     ⊙←⊙ ⎬   ⎨ 373   if →⊙↓↓ = ?
     ⊠←⊠ ⎪   ⎪ 361
     ⊗→⊗ ⎭   ⎩ 161

A) 6311   B) 5311   C) 4311   D) 1163   E) 3511

20. ⊗⊗● ⎫   ⎧ 933
     ↑↑↓ ⎪   ⎪ 995
     ↑↓↓ ⎬   ⎨ 211   if ⊗●↑⊙ = ?
     ●●⊗ ⎪   ⎪ 221
     ●⊙⊙ ⎭   ⎩ 559

A) 5912   B) 5923   C) 5913   D) 3295   E) 4923

TEST 41

1. $a \square b \rightarrow (2a + 3b) - (3a + 2b)$
    $8 \square 4 \rightarrow ?$
    A) 4   B) 6   C) -4   D) -4   E) 7

2. $x \odot y = x^y + y^x$
    $3 \odot 2 = ?$
    A) 17   B) 18   C) 24   D) 30   E) 32

3.    ?

4. | | | |
    |---|---|---|
    | □□□□
△△△
✱✱ | □□□
△△
✱✱✱ | □□
△
✱✱✱✱ |
    | □□
△△△△
✱ | □
△△△
✱✱ | △△
✱✱✱ |
    | □□□□□
△△
✱✱✱ | ? | □□□
✱✱✱✱✱ |

    A) □□□
△
✱✱✱✱

    B) □□□□
△△
✱✱✱✱

    C) □□□
△△
✱✱✱✱

    D) □□□□
△
✱✱✱✱

    E) □□□□□
△
✱✱✱

5.

    A)   B)   C)   D)   E)

6. → 5; 2   → 6; 6

   → 9; 6   → ?

   A) 6; 3   B) 6; 4   C) 6; 5   D) 6; 1   E) 6; 2

7. $\begin{array}{cc} a & b \\ 2 & 3 \\ + & + \\ \hline b & c \end{array}$ $c < 10$, $b + c = ?$

   A) 10   B) 12   C) 13   D) 14   E) 15

8.

   A) 32   B) 42   C) 41   D) 38   E) 48

9. $\dfrac{abab}{ab} + \dfrac{aaaa}{aa} = ?$

   A) 102   B) 202   C) 222   D) 122   E) 201

10. $\begin{array}{cc} ab & ab \\ ba & ba \\ + & - \\ \hline 132 & 18 \end{array}$ $a \cdot b = ?$

    A) 30   B) 32   C) 33   D) 35   E) 40

11.
$$\begin{array}{r} ab \\ ba \\ + \\ \hline 143 \end{array}$$

$a + b = 13$

$a \cdot b = ?$

A) 40   B) 42   C) 44   D) 48   E) 50

12.

4	6	8	10	2
5	7	9	x	

$x = ?$

A) 3   B) 4   C) 5   D) 6   E) 7

13.

19	12	10	6	2
7	2	4	x	

$x = ?$

A) 4   B) 5   C) 6   D) 7   E) 8

14.

▲	a	b	c
a			16
b	18		
c		14	

$a + b - c = ?$

A) 10   B) 12   C) 11   D) 13   E) 15

15.

✳	4	7	9
1	4	7	9
6	9	12	14
8	?	?	?

A) 12, 14, 17   B) 12, 17, 16   C) 11, 16, 17
D) 12, 15, 17   E) 11, 14, 16

16. $\begin{smallmatrix} & 2 & \\ 7 & \times & 3 \\ & 5 & \end{smallmatrix}$ $\begin{smallmatrix} & 11 & \\ 19 & \times & 13 \\ & 17 & \end{smallmatrix}$ $\begin{smallmatrix} & 23 & \\ x & \times & 29 \\ & 31 & \end{smallmatrix}$ x = ?

A) 30   B 32   C) 33   D) 36   E) 37

17.

✳	3	8	6	5
6	–	14	12	
7	10	–	–	11
8	–	16	14	–
4	?	?	?	?

What numbers should come where question mark?

A) –, 12, 10, –   B) –, 12, 10, 11   C) –, 11, 12, 10
D) 12, –, 10, 11   E) –, 11, 12, 13

18.
a b
a c   a + b + c = ?
$\dfrac{x\ x}{b\ b}$

A) 13   B) 14   C) 15   D)16   E) 17

19.
aa
bb   aa
$\dfrac{cc}{198}^{+}$ $\dfrac{bb}{cc}^{+}$ a + b = ?

A) 9   B) 8   C) 7   D) 6   E) 5

20.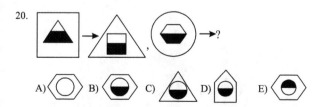

TEST 42

1.

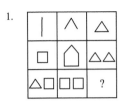

A) △△ B) □□ C) ⬡△ D) □□□ E) ⬡⬡

2.

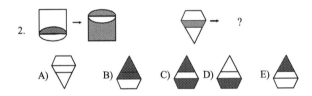

3.

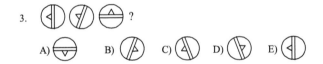

4. Find the different picture.

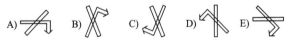

7. Find the different picture.

8.

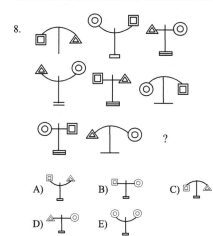

A) 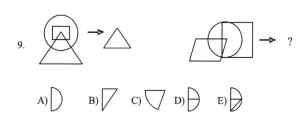   B)   C)

D)   E)

9.

A) B) C) D) E)

10.

A) B) C) D) E)

11.
$\triangle + \square + \odot = 4 + 5 + 3$

$\odot + \triangle + \blacksquare = 3 + 4 + 6$

$\square + \blacksquare + \odot = 5 + 6 + 3$

$\dfrac{\triangle + \square}{\blacksquare} = ?$

A) 2   B) 3   C) 4   D) $\dfrac{5}{2}$ E) $\dfrac{6}{4}$

12.

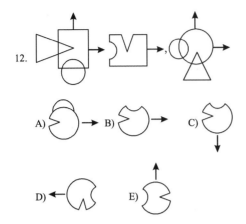

13.

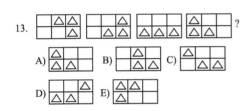

14.

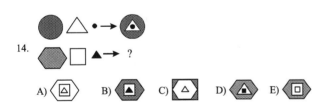

15.

	I	II	III
L	⌐	˥	Γ
V	?	∧	∧
E	Ǝ	?	E

A) ∨E   B) ∨Ǝ   C) ∧E   D) E∨   E) ∨E

16.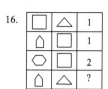

A) 1   B) 2   C) 3   D) 4   E) 0

17.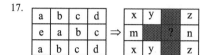

A) | | x | |
   | y | m |
   | | n | |

B) | | n | |
   | z | y |
   | | n | |

C) | | n | |
   | x | y |
   | | n | |

D) | | n | |
   | y | z |
   | | n | |

E) | | x | |
   | n | z |
   | | y |

18.

▲	abc	bcd	cde
amn	a		
mcd	c	cd	cd
kfe			?

A) a   B) b   C) c   D) de   E) e

19.

A) ▽   B) ◭   C) ◭   D) △   E) ◭

20.

A) ⊖   B) ⊘   C) ⊘   D) ⊘   E) ⊘

TEST 43

1. Find the different picture.

2.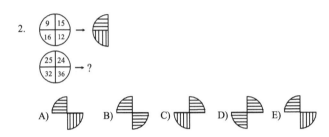

3. Find the different picture.

4. Find the different picture.

5.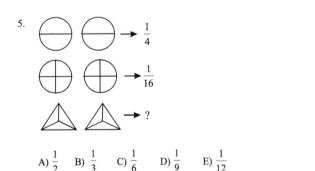

6.
$$\left.\begin{array}{l} \pi\ \alpha\ \pi\ \alpha\ \pi \\ \wedge\vee\wedge\vee\wedge \\ \#=\#=\# \\ \pi\wedge\pi\wedge\pi \\ \alpha\odot\alpha\odot\alpha \end{array}\right\}\ \#=\#=\#=?$$

A) 21212   B) 70707   C) 64646
D) 13131   E) 26262

7.

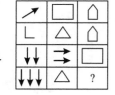

A) ∧∧∧   B) 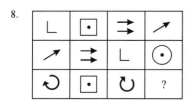   C) ⩾⩽⩾   D) ☐☐☐   E) ⩾⩾⩾

8.

A) ↻   B) ↓↓   C) ⌐   D) ▣   E) ⊙

9.

A) △   B) ☐   C) ⌂   D) ‖   E) ⬡

10.

A) ∧∨   B) ℧   C) ⊓⊓   D) ↓   E) ↟↟

11.

α	●	∅
v	⊙	v
π	∅	α
?	●	π

A) ○   B) ∅   C) ⊗   D) π   E) ⊙

12.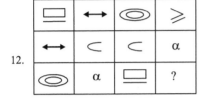

A) ≤   B) ⋀   C) α   D) ≥   E) ▭

13.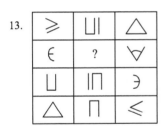

A) ∀   B) △   C) ∈   D) ⊓   E) △

14.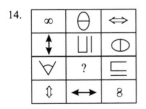

A) ⊖   B) ⊑   C) 8   D) △   E) ◁

15.

A) ⊖ B) ⓘ C) ⊜ D) ○→ E) ←○

16.

A) ▭ B) ⊞ C) ▭▭ D) ⊟ E) ⊞

17. Find the different picture.

A) △ B) ⇉ C) ⌂ D) ▱ E) ⬡

18. Find the different picture.

A) ‿ B) ↗ C) ▭ D) ⋈ E) ÷

19. Find the different picture.

A) ⇉ B) ↑↑ C) ↗ D) ↓↓ E) ⇆

20. 4, 7, 5, 8, 6, 9, 7, x   x = ?
    A) 10   B) 11   C) 12   D) 13   E) 14

TEST 44

1. Find the different picture.

   A) ╁   B) ✳   C) ╪   D) ⭐   E) ✳

2. 8, 12, 10, 14, 12, 16, x   x = ?
   A) 12   B) 13   C) 14   D) 16   E) 15

3. 7, 64, 8, 81, 9, 100, 10, x   x = ?
   A) 110   B) 121   C) 131   D) 141   E) 161

4.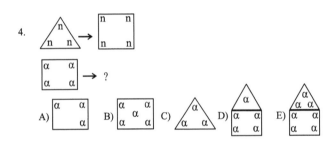

5. 64 ■ 21 → 10;3
   32 ■ 63 → 5;9
   61 ■ 44 → ?
   A) 10; 5   B) 10; 6   C) 11; 5   D) 5; 11   E) 7; 8

6. 74 ▲ 14 → 284
   64 ▲ 73 → 24 21
   36 ▲ 49 → 18 36
   99 ▲ 66 → ? ?
   A) 8116   B) 8137   C) 8136   D) 8172   E) 3681

7. $21\odot32 \rightarrow 35$

    $32\odot43 \rightarrow 57$

    $76\odot54 \rightarrow ?$

    A) 129   B) 139   C) 149   D) 921   E) 143

8. 128   (7, 5)   198
    144   (25, 5) 42
    162   (x)   64

    A) $\dfrac{19}{2}$ B) $\dfrac{19}{4}$ C) $\dfrac{19}{5}$ D) 19   E) 38

9. Find the different picture.

    A)   B)   C)   D)   E)

10. Find the different picture.

    A)   B)   C)   D)   E)

11. Find the different picture.

    A)   B)   C)   D)   E)

12.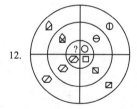

    What number should come where question mark?

    A)   B)   C)   D)   E)

13. $\left.\begin{array}{l}\square+\triangle=7\\ \oslash+\triangle=8\\ \square+\oslash=9\end{array}\right\}$ isə $\triangle+\square+\oslash=?$

    A) 10   B) 11   C) 12   D) 13 E) 15

14.
$$\frac{\substack{aa \\ +bb}}{132}$$
a-b=2 and a·b=?

    A) 36   B) 32   C) 30   D) 35   E) 36

15. △⊖□△⊖○□△⊖☑□△○?□△▲☑△⊖
    What number should come where question mark?

    A) △   B) ○   C) □   D) ⊖   E) ■

16. $a^2 \blacksquare b^2 \rightarrow a+b$
    $9\blacksquare 4 \rightarrow 5$
    $16\blacksquare 25 \rightarrow ?$

    A) 8   B) 9   C) 10   D) 12   E) 13

17.  ?

    A) ⊕   B) ⊕   C) ⟠   D) ⊗   E) △

18.

△	△	⬡
△	∧	⬠
□	∧	?

    A) △   B) □   C) ∨   D) ⌂   E) ⬡

19. A: 6   4   3   2
    B: 37 17 8   3
    C: 3   4   5   7
    D: ?   ?   ?   ?

    A) 9, 17, 24, 48   B) 8, 16, 25, 49   C) 8, 11, 17, 49   D) 8, 15, 17, 26   E) 10, 17, 24, 48

20. A: 142, 642, 524, 716
    B: 6, 11, 10, 13
    C: 124, 147, 781, 114
    D: ?, ?, ?, ?

    A) 6, 11, 15, 5   B) 6, 11, 14, 4   C) 6, 11, 16, 6
    D) 7, 12, 16, 6   E) 7, 12, 16, 7

TEST 45

1.
$$\left. \begin{array}{l} \triangle + \square = 25 \\ \square - \triangle = 1 \\ \triangle - \blacktriangle = 3 \end{array} \right\} \triangle + \square + \blacktriangle = ?$$

   A) 32   B) 33   C) 34   D) 36   E) 38

2.
$$\begin{array}{r} aa \\ \underline{\times bb} \\ \cdots \\ \underline{+\ \cdots} \\ 1452 \end{array}$$
   $(a+b)^2 = ?$

   A) 36   B) 49   C) 82   D) 68   E) 100

3. $A\dfrac{|5}{|B}$ $B\dfrac{|6}{|C}$ $A\dfrac{|30}{}$ $D = ?$

   $-\dfrac{}{2}$ $-\dfrac{}{1}$ $-\dfrac{}{D}$

   A) 2   B) 3   C) 5   D) 7   E) 4

4.   10, 12, 32, 34, ?
   A) 18   B) 47   C) 39   D) 42   E) 44

5.   110, 130, 141, 116, ?

   A) 721   B) 182   C) 183   D) 191   E)169

6.   74   82   92   86
   44   20   22   ?
   A) 80   B) 81   C) 82   D) 84   E) 88

7.   43 → 7,   73 → ?
   62 → 32,
   82 → 60
   A) 25   B) 30   C) 35   D) 36   E) 40

8.   x = ?

    A) 10   B) 12   C) 13   D) 14   E) 16

9.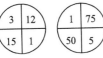

    A) 2   B) 3   C) 4   D) 6   E) 7

10. 19, 23, 29, 31, ?
    A) 33   B) 34   C) 35   D) 36   E) 37

11. 13, 15, 18, 22, 27, ?
    A) 30   B) 31   C) 33   D) 34   E) 35

12. $124 \rightarrow 3$
    $622 \rightarrow 31$
    $444 \rightarrow 11$
    $662 \rightarrow ?$
    A) 30   B) 31   C) 32   D) 33   E) 34

13. $842 \rightarrow 10$
    $953 \rightarrow 11$
    $444 \rightarrow 4$
    $662 \rightarrow ?$
    A) 10   B) 11   C) 12   D) 13   E) 14

14. I $m \triangle n = m^2 + n^2 + mn$
    II $m \blacktriangle n = m^2 + n^2 - mn$
    III $\left(\dfrac{1}{6} \triangle \dfrac{1}{6} \right) \blacktriangle \dfrac{1}{6} = ?$

    A) $\dfrac{1}{144}$ B) $\dfrac{1}{36}$ C) $\dfrac{1}{48}$ D) $\dfrac{1}{38}$ E) $\dfrac{1}{68}$

15.

+	a	b	c
a			
b	c+2		
c			24

a + b + c = ?

A) 22   B) 24   C) 26   D) 28   E) 30

16. 123□ →224
    234□ →335
    783□ →?
    A) 784   B) 884   C) 885   D) 886   E) 887

17. 234■ →5
    149■ →5
    924■ →34
    428■ →?
    A) 30   B) 32   C) 34   D) 36   E) 38

18.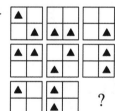

A)   B)   C)   D)   E)

19. A: 282, 602, 404, 905
    B: 14, 30, 10, 18
    C: 122, 805, 762, 963
    D: ?, ?, ?, ?
    A) 6, 26, 38, 23   B) 6, 18, 48, 24   C) 7, 18, 48, 24
    D) 8, 16, 48, 26   E) 6, 16, 38, 32

20. 9362 → 24
    7241 → 15
    9421 → 15
    6183 → ?
    A) 20   B) 24   C) 25   D) 26   E) 30

TEST 46

1. $234\square \rightarrow 6,12,9,24$
   $154\square \rightarrow 5,20,10,20$
   $354\square \rightarrow ?$

   A) 15, 20, 12, 50   B) 15, 20, 12, 60   C) 15, 16, 12, 60
   D) 20, 15, 12, 60   E) 24, 15, 12, 60

2.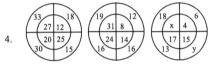

   A)   B)   C)   D)   E)

3. 12, 13, 14, 14, 18, 17, 24, 22, 32, ?

   A) 26   B) 27   C) 28   D) 29   E) 30

4.

   $x + y = ?$
   A) 27   B) 28   C) 30   D) 35   E) 40

5.

   $x + y = ?$
   A) $\dfrac{127}{2}$ B) $\dfrac{285}{4}$ C) $\dfrac{385}{4}$ D) $\dfrac{195}{6}$ E) $\dfrac{395}{4}$

6. $243\blacksquare \rightarrow 27$
   $366\blacksquare \rightarrow 42$
   $643\bigcirc \rightarrow 49$
   $427\bigcirc \rightarrow 31$
   $(998\blacksquare)\bigcirc \rightarrow ?$

   A) 18   B) 81   C) 8   D) 80   E) 9

7.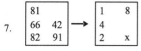

x = ?

A) 1   B) 2   C) 3   D) 6   E) 9

8.   6, 7, 9, 11, 12, 15, 15, 19, 18, ?

A) 20   B) 21   C) 22   D) 23   E) 24

9.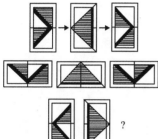

?

A)   B)   C)   D)   E)

10.

A) 8   B) 7   C) 6   D) 5   E) 4

11.

A) 5   B) 6   C) 7   D) 8   E) 9

12.

*	12	15	16
2	□	△	□
3	□	□	△
4	A	B	C

A) 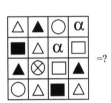　B) △△□　　　C) □△□

D) □□△　　E) □□□

13.

 =?

A) 1257　B) 1257　C) 1257　D) 1257　E) 5147
　4273　　4173　　4273　　4173　　2032
　2032　　2032　　2032　　3042　　2273
　5147　　5141　　4147　　5131　　1257

14. Find the different picture.

A) 　B) 　C)

D) 　E)

15.

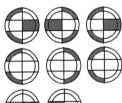

?

A) 　B) 　C) 　D) ...　E) ...

16. 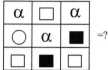 =?

A) 132
212
331

B) 121
212
343

C) 121
314
242

D) 123
214
123

E) 212
134
321

17. 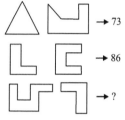 → 73

→ 86

→ ?

A) 510   B) 410   C) 310   D) 710   E) 610

18. Find the different picture.

A)   B)   C)   D)   E)

19. 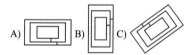  → ?

A)   B)   C)   D)   E)

20. Find the different picture.

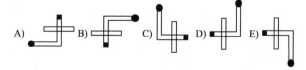

A)   B)   C)   D)   E)

TEST 47

1. Find the different picture.

2.

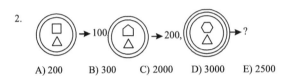

A) 200   B) 300   C) 2000   D) 3000   E) 2500

3.

▮ 3 3	3 3 ━━ 4	3 ▮ 4 3 ▮ 4
4 ━━ 3 3	4 ▮ 3 4 ▮ 3	3 3 ━━ 4 4 4
3 ▮ 4 3 ▮ 4	4 4 4 ━━ 3 3	?

A) 3
━━━━
4444   B) 4 ▮ 3
4
4 ▮ 3   C) 4
━━
3   D) 4 ▮ 3
4 ▮ 3   E) 4 ▮ 3
4
4
4 ▮ 3

4.

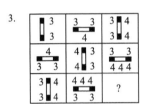

What picture should come where question mark?

A) □○   B) □□   C) ○○   D) □○○   E) □□○

5.   45781   ┐   ┌ ▬ ▲ △ ✳ ●
     45631   │   │ ⊠ ▲ ▬ ✳ △
     13734   ⟩   ⟨ ⊠ ▲ ● ○ △
     13457   │   │ △ ○ ▬ ● ⊠
     75186   ┘   └ △ ○ ⊠ ▲ ▬

✳ + △ + □ + ○ + ▲ = ?

A) 19   B) 20   C) 21   D) 22   E) 23

6.

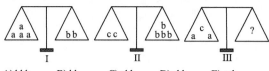

A) bbb   B) bb   C) cbb   D) abb   E) ccb

7. □△⊠○▲) (■●⊗■∗   ▲○⊠△□ =?
    ○⊠△□▲ | | ○∗●■■
    ▲○⊠△□ }| ■■●∗⊗
    ⊠▲△○□ | | ∗●■■⊗
    □⊠▲△○) (●⊗■∗■

    A) ■●⊗■∗   B) ○∗●■■   C) ■■●∗⊗

    D) ●■■⊗   E) ●⊗■∗■

8.

A) 96   B) 66   C) 88   D) 77   E) 99

9. Find the different picture.

    A) ⊔⌐   B) ℂ   C) ℤ   D) ℂ̲   E) ⋀

10.

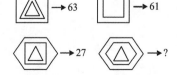

A) 108   B) 701   C) 601   D) 801   E) 198

11.
$$\begin{array}{cccc} a & b & c & a \\ +b & +c & +d & +c \\ \hline 14 & 11 & 13 & 15 \end{array} \qquad d = ?$$

A) 5   B) 6   C) 7   D) 8   E) 9

12.
$$\begin{array}{l} abc \\ abc \\ abc \\ abc \\ +abc \\ \hline 1375 \end{array} \qquad a \cdot b \cdot c = ?$$

A) 30   B) 40   C) 50   D) 60   E) 70

13.

+	a	b	c
a	b		16
b		4a	
c			6a

$\dfrac{a+b}{c} = ?$

A) 1   B) 2   C) 3   D) 4   E) 5

14.

x	a	b	c
a		12	36
b			48
c			

$a \cdot b - c = ?$

A) 3   B) 2   C) 1   D) 0   E) -2

15.

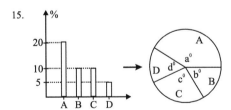

$a^0 = ?, b^0 = ?, c^0 = ?, d^0 = ?$

	A	B	C	D
A)	170	80	80	50
B)	160	80	80	20
C)	160	80	70	40
D)	160	80	80	30
E)	160	80	80	40

16.

*	18	14	15	12
6	□	△	△	□
4	△	△	△	□
3	□	△	?	?

A) △△   B) □□   C) □△   D) △□   E) -△

17.
$$abb$$
$$*\ 77$$
$$\overline{.....}$$
$$.......$$
$$\underline{+\qquad}$$
$$49588$$

$$ab$$
$$ba$$
$$\underline{+\qquad}$$
$$?$$

A) 140   B) 141   C) 142   D) 143   E) 146

18. $64▲22 \to 2$
$83▲21 \to 6$
$94▲31 \to 7$
$91▲81 \to ?$

A) 10   B) 12   C) 13   D) 14   E) 15

19.

$\begin{array}{c|c} A+1 & B-1 \\ \hline & 3 \\ 2 & \end{array}$ $\begin{array}{c|c} B+1 & c-1 \\ \hline & 4 \\ 3 & \end{array}$

A) 8c - 12   B) 8c + 12   C) 12c - 8
D) 12c + 8   E) 12c + 10

20.

$m^0 = ?$
A) 100   B) 110   C) 120   D) 140   E) 160

TEST 48

1.

A) 12   B) 14   C) 16   D) 18   E) 20

2.
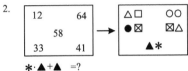

$* \cdot \blacktriangle + \blacktriangle$ =?

A) 33   B) 45   C) 48   D) 52   E) 63

3.

x = ?

A) 2   B) 3   C) 4   D) 6   E) 7

4.
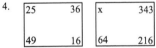

x = ?

A) 120   B) 124   C) 316   D) 217   E) 125

5. Find the different picture.

A)   B)   C)   D)   E)

6.
$$\begin{array}{r} +\ aa \\ bb \\ cc \\ dd \\ ee \\ \hline 165 \end{array}$$
and $a+b+c+d+e=?$

A) 11   B) 12   C) 13   D) 14   E) 15

7. 62▲43 → 87
    44▲12 → 83
    24▲21 → 63
    61▲16 → ?
    A) 77   B) 66   C) 55   D) 68   E) 86

8. 42 74 18 65
    51 83 27 ?
    A) 74   B) 72   C) 56   D) 57   E) 66

9.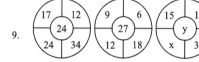

    x + y = ?
    A 27   B) 37   C) 47   D) 57   E) 67

10. 12   7   7   12
    20   4   18   6
    9   11   12   8
    8   12   6   x
    x = ?
    A) 14   B) 13   C) 12   D) 11   E) 10

11.   . . .   K = ?
         x 53
         . . . .
        2250
      + ____
        ..K..

    A) 2   B) 3   C) 4   D) 6   E) 8

12. 6376   3493 5492 7564
    1842   1227 2018 ?

    A) 3623   B) 3524   C) 4232   D) 4223   E) 6436

13.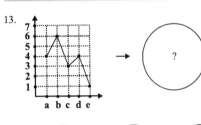

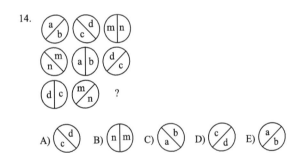

A) ... B) ... C) ...

D) ... E) ...

14.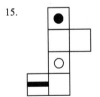

A) ... B) ... C) ... D) ... E) ...

15.

A) ... B) ... C) ... D) ... E) ...

16.

6	4	2
8	1	6
12	2	2
x	1	16

$x = ?$

A) 1   B) 2   C) 3   D) 4   E) 6

17.   ABC $A \times B \times C = ?$
    ABC
    ABC
    ABC
    ABC
    +
    ‾‾‾‾‾‾‾
    46BC

A) 50   B) 60   C) 70   D) 80   E) 90

18. Find the different picture.

A)   B)   C)    D)   E)

19. Choose the correct answer.

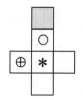

A)   B)   C)   D)   E)

20. 2, 5, 9, 14, 20, ?

A) 22   B) 23   C) 24   D) 27   E) 28

TEST 49

1.

a	b	c

I

	c	b
	a	

II

c		
		b
		a

III

c	a	
	b	

IV → ?

A)

	a	
	b	
c		

B)

a		
c		
	b	

C)

a		
c	b	

D)

	c	
	b	a

E)

b		
c		a

2. 23, 29, 31, 37, ?
    A) 41   B) 42   C) 44   D) 46   E) 48

3. 123□ → 6, 144□ → 16,
    323□ → 18, 455□ → ?
    A) 70   B) 80   C) 90   D) 100   E) 102

4. 123□ → 4
    444□ → 11
    522□ → 26
    243□ → ?
    A) 5   B) 6   C) 7   D) 8   E) 10

5. 334⊞ → 10
    123⊞ → 6
    962⊞ → 17
    873⊞ → ?
    A) 12   B) 13   C) 14   D) 18   E) 20

6. △ → 5; 4, ⊞ → 7; 6
    ⊠ → 6; 4, ⬚ → ?
    A) 7, 4   B) 7, 3   C) 7, 2   D) 6, 4   E) 6, 5

7. 10, 13, 12, 15, 14, 17, ?
   A) 16   B) 17   C) 18   D) 19   E) 20

8.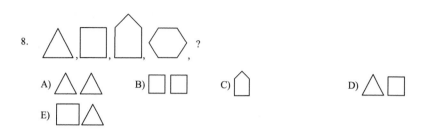

   A) 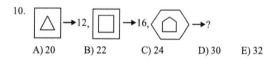   B) (squares)   C) (house)   D) (triangle square)

   E) (square triangle)

9.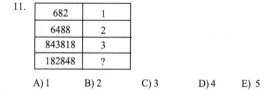

   A) 123   B) 454   C) 523   D) 414   E) 416

10.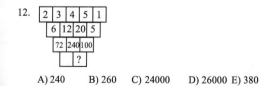

    A) 20   B) 22   C) 24   D) 30   E) 32

11.

682	1
6488	2
843818	3
182848	?

   A) 1   B) 2   C) 3   D) 4   E) 5

12.

2	3	4	5	1
6	12	20	5	
72	240	100		
?				

   A) 240   B) 260   C) 24000   D) 26000   E) 380

13.

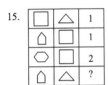

A) ⊖ B) ⊘ C) ⊗ D) ⓪ E) ◯

14. □64 → 12
    □83 → 12
    □92 → 9
    □74 → ?
    A) 28 B) 14   C) 7   D) 8   E) 16

15.

A) 1   B) 2   C) 3   D) 4   E) 0

16. Find the different picture.

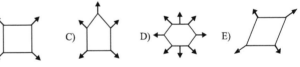

A)   B)   C)   D)   E)

17.

*	3	4	5
1	△	□	△
2	□	△	□
3	△	a	b

ab = ?

A) △△   B) □□   C) □△   D) △□   E) △

18.

9	11	8	12
6	14	15	5
3	17	1	19
13	7	6	x

x = ?

A) 10   B) 12   C) 13   D) 14   E) 16

19.

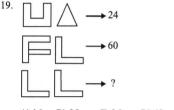

→ 24

→ 60

→ ?

A) 16   B) 25   C) 36   D) 42   E) 44

20.

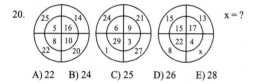

x = ?

A) 22   B) 24   C) 25   D) 26   E) 28

AUTHOR

Tayyip oral is a graduate of Qafqaz University.He has written many books about math and intelligence questions.he formerly taught math and IQ classes at Baku Araz preparatory school.Since 2011 he has been living in the US.

PUBLICATIONS

- T. Oral, E. Seyidzade, , Araz publishing, Master's Degree Program Preparation (IQ), Cag Ogretim, Araz Courses, Baku, Azerbaijan, 2010.

A master's degree program preparation text book for undergraduate students in Azerbaijan.

- T. oral,M. Aranli, F. Sadigov, ,and N. Resullu, Resullu publishing, Baku, Azerbaijan - 2012 (3.edition)

A text book for job placement exam in Azerbaijan for undergraduate and post undergraduate students in Azerbaijan.

- T. Oral and I. Hesenov, Algebra (Text book), Nurlar Printing and Publishing, Baku, Azerbaijan, 2001.

A text book covering algebra concepts and questions with detailed explanations at high school level in Azerbaijan.

- T. Oral, I. Hesenov, S. Maharramov, and J. Mikaylov, Geometry (Text book), Nurlar Printing and Publishing, Baku, Azerbaijan, 2002.

A text book for high school students to prepare them for undergraduate education in Azerbaijan.

- T. Oral, I. Hesenov, and S. Maharramov, Geometry Formulas (Text Book), Araz courses, Baku, Azerbaijan, 2003.

A text book for high school students' university exam preparation in Azerbaijan.

- T. Oral, I. Hesenov, and S. Maharramov, Algebra Formulas (Text Book), Araz courses, Baku, Azerbaijan, 2000

A university exam preparation text book for high school students in Azerbaijan.

Answers

	1	2	3	4	5	6	7	8	9	10	11	12	13	14	15	16	17	18	19	20
Quiz1	E	D	D	D	B	D	E	E	E	D	D	D	B	E	A	C	A	B	B	A
Quiz2	E	C	A	D	D	D	C	D	D	C	E	B	D	D	C	B	D	E	A	B
Quiz3	C	D	E	A	A	E	A	A	E	D	A	D	E	C	D	A	C	B	B	B
Quiz4	A	D	C	D	A	A	D	E	E	A	E	D	E	B	D	B	E	C	D	D
Test-1	E	D	B	B	B	A	C	A	B	C	C	A	E	E	C	B	B	B	B	A
Test-2	D	E	B	A	A	B	E	A	D	A	A	A	E	D	A	A	E	C	D	A
Test-3	D	D	C	A	D	E	D	D	D	C	E	B	C	E	E	D	E	E	E	C
Test-4	B	E	D	A	E	D	B	A	B	C	E	B	C	A	B	C	B	C	B	D
Test-5	B	D	E	C	D	D	B	B	D	B	B	E	C	C	C	D	D	D	D	D
Test-6	B	E	B	C	C	C	A	B	C	C	D	A	C	E	D	D	C	D	B	A
Test-7	D	B	B	D	A	D	A	A	E	E	D	C	D	D	E	B	D	C	E	D
Test-8	C	E	D	A	D	E	C	A	A	C	C	D	C	C	A	A	E	C	D	C
Test-9	E	B	A	D	C	B	B	C	B	E	D	A	B	C	C	C	E	C	A	C
Test-10	D	C	D	D	D	C	B	C	E	B	D	B	E	A	C	A	A	B	A	A
Test-11	B	A	D	C	E	E	B	A	D	B	B	D	D	A	A	D	A	E	A	A
Test-12	D	E	D	B	B	B	C	C	C	B	D	C	C	C	C	A	E	C	A	E
Test-13	E	B	D	C	D	A	E	B	A	E	C	D	D	C	B	C	B	E	C	B
Test-14	A	B	C	C	C	E	D	C	C	C	B	B	D	D	B	A	B	D	C	C
Test-15	C	C	C	E	C	A	E	C	B	A	A	A	D	D	A	E	E	E	E	B
Test-16	B	E	C	B	D	B	D	A	E	B	C	C	B	D	A	A	B	B	D	D
Test-17	E	A	C	A	B	A	E	E	D	B	C	E	C	A	B	A	E	E	B	B
Test-18	B	D	D	E	D	D	E	E	E	E	E	B	C	C	D	D	E	C	E	E
Test-19	C	B	E	B	B	A	D	A	D	B	D	E	B	C	E	A	C	D	E	B
Test-20	B	D	D	D	A	B	C	C	A	C	E	E	D	B	D	D	E	B	B	E
Test-21	C	B	A	E	A	E	C	C	D	D	B	A	B	A	D	C	A	E	B	D
Test-22	D	B	D	E	C	B	B	E	A	C	A	C	A	C	E	D	D	C	C	A
Test-23	A	A	C	C	E	B	C	A	C	A	E	B	C	D	C	A	C	A	C	C
Test-24	E	E	D	D	D	A	C	E	D	E	C	E	B	E	D	E	B	E	A	E

Test-25	E	E	E	A	E	E	E	B	A	E	C	B	D	A	C	E	B	E	E	E
Test-26	D	E	B	D	B	B	E	A	C	B	C	D	D	C	B	B	C	E	C	E
Test-27	E	B	D	D	D	E	B	B	D	A	A	B	D	C	A	C	C	A	E	E
Test-28	D	B	B	A	A	B	D	D	B	A	E	B	B	B	D	D	B	E	C	C
Test-29	A	B	A	A	B	A	C	C	E	B	E	C	E	E	B	A	E	E	E	D
Test-30	E	A	E	A	C	A	E	A	E	E	B	B	A	A	B	B	C	E	D	A
Test-31	C	C	A	D	E	E	B	D	E	C	A	B	E	E	D	D	D	B	A	D
Test-32	B	D	A	B	A	E	D	B	E	C	E	B	C	E	A	E	C	A	B	A
Test-33	B	D	D	A	C	B	E	D	A	E	E	E	E	C	D	B	E	C	B	E
Test-34	D	A	E	B	D	E	E	B	E	B	B	C	D	C	C	D	C	A	C	E
Test-35	E	D	A	E	C	B	C	C	D	E	C	D	D	D	B	A	A	B	E	A
Test-36	C	B	C	E	E	A	B	B	D	D	C	E	D	E	B	B	E	E	C	D
Test-37	B	B	D	E	A		B	A	B	C	A	E	D	E	B	E	B	B	D	B
Test-38	E	B	D	C	A	D	D	A	E	D	D	D	B	B	A	B	D	E	E	E
Test-39	C	B	C	C	E	C	E	E	C	C	A	B	C	B	E	E	A	E	A	D
Test-40	B	B	A	D	E	E	B	E	B	B	C	C	B	A	A	A	C	A	A	B
Test-41	C	A	E	D	D	B	E	A	B	B	B	D	A	B	E	E	A	A	A	B
Test-42	C	C	D	D			D	A	B	B	E	B	E	B	B	B	C	E	C	D
Test-43	D	A	E	E	D	B	E	E	E	E	D	E	E	B	B	B	C	E	C	A
Test-44	E	C	B	D	E	C	B	A	D	C	E	A	C	D		B	B	E	D	A
Test-45	C	B	D	E	A	D	E	B	C	E	E	D	A	A	C	B	A	D	E	C
Test-46	B	E	D	A	C	C	E	D	D	A	C	E	E	B	C	C	A	E	D	D
Test-47	C	B	E	A	C	B	B	A	C	D	C	E	A	D	E	B	C	E	C	C
Test-48	D	D	A	E	E	E	A	A	C	A	E	B	C	C	A	C	E	E	A	D
Test-49	C	A	D	D	D	A	A	D	A	D	C	C	E	B	B	D	C	D	C	D

IQ
Intelligence questions
For
Middle school students
High school students